PRAISE FOR *DISCIPLINE WITHOUT DAMAGE*

"In *Discipline Without Damage*, Dr. Vanessa Lapointe explores the important question of *why we discipline rather than just how*. We need to question the notion that the only way to raise happy, capable and caring future adults is to punish children when they don't behave according to our wishes. In fact, by showing that children really need kindness, fairness and a caring, safe environment, Dr. Lapointe has created a trustworthy resource for parents."

Maggie Dent

Author of *9 Things: A Back-to Basics Guide to Calm, Common-sense, Connected Parenting Birth–8*

"This book is a must-read for all parents who know what feels right about disciplining their kids, but have been advised to do the opposite. Dr. Lapointe combines scientific theory with her wealth of experience working with children, and gives clear examples of how to put it all into practice. Read this book and see the results in your happy, well-adjusted child."

Barbara Fitzgerald M.D. FRCP(C)

Developmental pediatrician

Clinical associate professor, University of British Columbia

"In *Discipline without Damage*, Dr. Lapointe shows why communication and connection are so important for our children. And why it is especially important for us adults to discipline ourselves so that we don't go down the path of disconnection in the name of good behavior. Read this book and discover creative ways to be with your children and respect them for who they are."

Vikram Vij

Chef, sommelier, and co-owner of Vij's group of companies

"I love this book! It's a rare combination of science-based, practical, respectful, and effective discipline."

Dr. Tina Payne Bryson, PhD

Co-author of the *New York Times* bestselling books *The Whole-Brain Child* and *No-Drama Discipline*

"In this eloquent book, Dr. Lapointe makes a powerful case for disciplining our children without power struggles, manipulation or control. An insightful guide for all parents!"

Dr. Shefali Tsabary, PhD

Author of the *New York Times* bestselling book *The Conscious Parent*

"Dr. Lapointe has given parents, family members and the professionals who work with them a wonderful gift. *Discipline Without Damage* should be required reading for us all. Written from a deep pool of experience and knowledge, this practical book helps us understand what children need to thrive."

Dana Brynelsen, OBC, LLD

Former provincial advisor, Infant Development Program of BC

DISCIPLINE
WITHOUT
DAMAGE

HOW TO GET
YOUR KIDS TO BEHAVE
WITHOUT MESSING THEM UP

DR. VANESSA LAPOINTE, R. PSYCH

Cataloguing data available from Library and Archives Canada
ISBN 978-1-928055-10-5 (pbk)
ISBN 978-1-928055-11-2 (epub)
ISBN 978-1-928055-12-9 (PDF)

Published by LifeTree Media Ltd.
lifetreemedia.com

Distributed by Greystone Books Ltd.
greystonebooks.com

Editor: Michelle MacAleese
Designer: Ingrid Paulson
Author photo: Lindsay Faber Photography
Printed in Canada by Friesens

For my boys—big and small

CONTENTS

II CONNECTION IN ACTION

FOREWORD

I am excited that you are holding this book in your hands. I don't say that lightly. Every year, I read most of the parenting books that are published in English, and *Discipline Without Damage: How To Get Your Kids To Behave Without Messing Them Up,* by Dr. Vanessa Lapointe, is one of the five best parenting books that I've read in the past five years. Most child raising books tell you how to address the symptoms of your child's misbehavior, but never help you to address the cause of those symptoms—the child's inability to remain emotionally regulated in the face of the challenges he perceives in his life. As a result, they prescribe interventions that may stop the child's misbehavior in the moment, but actually erode your relationship with your child and make future misbehavior more likely. If you find yourself in a cycle of misbehavior and punishment that your heart tells you isn't the path to a more harmonious family, this is the book for you.

Many books on child raising leave parents feeling inadequate because they can't actually implement their advice, which tells them to keep the child under control. But that isn't the parent's fault. It's because most parenting "experts" ignore the role of emotions—both ours, and our children's. They imply that if parents will simply apply consistent "consequences," children will learn the right lessons and stop "willfully" misbehaving. But children don't misbehave because they enjoy it, or because they're bad, or because they don't know what they "should" do. All children want to be good, to stay in a state of warm connection to us, to "do the right thing." They misbehave because they're emotionally disregulated and don't know how to find a way to calm down and "do the right thing." So you may try to stay calm, firm and consistent, but what do you do when your child is too disregulated to comply with your directives? You may try to stand firm, but what can you do when your strong-willed child doesn't acquiesce to your "consequences" and things escalate to a full-blown power-struggle?

In this groundbreaking book, Lapointe cuts through the confusion about discipline and gives parents the clear answers they need. Since the cause of all human behavior is emotion, understanding and solving a child's difficult behaviors requires us to begin by helping the child to regulate her emotions. As Lapointe makes clear, children can't emotionally regulate until they feel safe, and that is only possible when we, the adults, regulate our own emotions and step up responsibly to take charge of the situation. Once you realize that your child's sense of safety is your priority, remaining connected to your child becomes your bottom line. Connection creates safety, which helps your child move back into a state of emotional regulation, from which she can "choose" to cooperate.

When you start reading this book, it seems to be about discipline. But *Discipline Without Damage* isn't about how to get your child to cooperate by using time-outs, consequences, threats, punishments, star charts, praise, or anything else that most of us think of as discipline. In fact, Lapointe's genius is in showing the reader how conventional discipline creates children who are needy, demanding, bossy, aggressive, and difficult. She argues convincingly that conventional discipline disconnects us from our child, thus triggering his attachment alarms. Since the child's need for our safe, emotionally responsive presence trumps all his other emotional needs, the child will always acquiesce and "try" to behave. Unfortunately, the main lesson children learn from conventional discipline is that our love for them is conditional, contingent on their ability to control their behavior. But since that makes the child feel even less safe, it makes future disregulation and misbehavior more likely. Since we aren't giving the child any help with the emotions driving the misbehavior, their cooperation is short-lived, and we're sucked back into what Lapointe calls the "discipline vortex."

Luckily, Lapointe has some helpful answers for parents, including recommendations on how parents can step up to be the leaders in their house—what she calls "hulking up." (Yes, that's a reference to the comic book character the Hulk, and that idea alone is worth the price of this book.) She also makes clear that far from being "permissive," this kind of parenting meets children's deeper needs for connection and safety, giving them an environment in which they can thrive.

I hope that this book makes it onto the short list of every parent. I think it can change the world.

Dr. Laura Markham, PhD
Founding editor of AhaParenting.com and
author of *Peaceful Parent, Happy Kids*

INTRODUCTION

One hot and stuffy Saturday afternoon I attended a wedding at which I was seated close to a young family with a 3-year-old girl. All that sitting still, keeping quiet, and wearing uncomfortable dress clothes can make a forty-five-minute ceremony a pressure cooker for kids—and for their parents. I couldn't help imagining how that little girl might have been feeling, and, more strongly, what the girl's parents might have been feeling.

As a parent in these situations, it can seem that all eyes are on you and your child while everybody assesses your family, deciding whether or not your child is a "good" child and, in turn, whether or not you are a "good" parent. You hope this *will not* be the day that your child melts down about not getting an extra cupcake. You hope this *will* be the day that your child manages to remain quiet through the entire ceremony. After all, we all want to be thought of as "good," and we also want others to look on our children as "good." But is a child who reaches the end of her rope and loses it because she doesn't get that extra cupcake really a "bad" child? Is the parent who has worked hard to distract and calm a child who has had to sit an extra long time and just can't manage it really a "bad" parent?

As I watched this little girl, I noticed something kind of peculiar: she was exceptionally quiet and still. I also noticed the accolades that both child and parents were receiving—clearly this was a "good" child and these were "good" parents. It struck me that there was a flaw in this logic. Maybe this girl just happened, temperamentally, to be very easy going and not at all fussed by the hoopla going on around her. Maybe this girl was fearful that there would be consequences to behavior that was anything other than what had been explained to her as "acceptable," i.e., quiet and sweet. Did her silence necessarily indicate that she is a "good" child? Was her silence evidence of "good" parenting? And what does "good" even imply—is it a moral standard or a practical one? Are we judging the child according to rules about behavior made up and enforced by adults, or are we judging the adults?

Regardless of the situation, it seems that when it comes to parenting and discipline there are always onlookers full of opinions about what "should" have happened and what "should" have been done. If the girl at the wedding had experienced a meltdown, I wonder what everybody would have been thinking then? Inevitably, many of the onlookers would have thought, if not whispered to each other, that she needed some discipline. Her parents would have been under pressure to step up and tell her that her behavior was "inappropriate." After all, isn't that what "good" parents would do? In turn, if she were a "good" child, then she would have had no trouble responding to the discipline by settling down.

The question is this: in such a situation, is it really "discipline" that is needed? Or, if we approach the meltdown through a more compassionate lens, informed by an understanding of what is normal for children at various ages and stages of development, might we see that little girl as just needing some cuddle time away from the crowd or some free time outside to blow off pent-up energy? Is childhood meant to be quiet and calm, or are there supposed to be flare-ups and blowouts to help children figure things out and get the chance to grow up in the best possible way? Are you a "bad" parent if you have a child who reacts as children simply will do? Are you a "bad" parent if you have a child who reacts more intensely than other children? And is the child in these cases really "bad" and really in need of discipline, or just in need of care and support?

Most parents are tired of feeling publicly judged. Amidst the general chaos of managing our day-to-day lives, we do not also want to be evaluated on our "parenting technique," so we strive to have our children appear well behaved to escape this judgment. However, our focus on demanding "good behavior" without cultivating a foundational understanding of what kids truly *need* to grow up in the best possible way is not only ineffective but potentially dangerous. We understand discipline as a way to get from children good behavior that demonstrates acceptance of social norms, but how this discipline is carried out is of ultimate importance in delivering to children what they *need*. This book will talk about what children need, what discipline is, and how you can deliver it without damage. Yes, we want our children to grow into beings who are capable of good behavior and who understand the limits of the world they live in. But we want that for them alongside healthy social-emotional development. We do not want to damage our children by trading off this healthy development for good behavior.

I have been working as a psychologist, educator, and lecturer for more than fifteen years, and of all the workshop requests I receive, discipline is by far the most popular topic. Big people everywhere want to know *how* to discipline. By "big people" I mean parents, grandparents, teachers, neighbors, aunties, uncles, caregivers, and any other adult who plays a significant role in the nurturing and growing up of a child. Big people want strategies and techniques. They want to make sure they are *doing* discipline correctly. I often wonder how discipline became the object of such fascination and focus in the dominant parenting culture when the growing numbers of anxiety-related conditions and the skyrocketing rate of depression in children would suggest that we have much greater issues to address.

Today, approximately 6 to 8 percent of children aged 5 to 17 years old have diagnosable anxiety-related conditions, such as generalized anxiety disorder, separation anxiety, phobias, panic disorder, and selective mutism. By the time they reach adulthood, this number has mushroomed to between 18 and 20 percent, suggesting that 1 in 5 of us will be diagnosable with an anxiety disorder at some point in our lifetime.[1] Similarly, children born today are ten times more likely than children born just 3 generations ago to be diagnosed with depression at some point in their lifetime.[2] The question is why. What has changed that is causing us to struggle so significantly with raising our children to be happy, healthy adults? This is a complex question that demands a carefully considered answer.

Some of what has set us on this collision course between our best intentions as big people and how significantly our children are struggling is that we have lost touch with the true *needs* of our children. Parenting is not easy. We raise our children in relative isolation compared with past generations,[3] we face escalating demands on our family time,[4] and we feel pressure to push our children to attain increasingly high levels of success at younger and younger ages to help them "make it" in this world.[5] We have become focused on so-called good behavior as the desired end result of our efforts. But, as a society, we are out of touch with what is truly important for our growing children: identifying their deeply rooted needs and compassionately setting up a healthy world in which those needs will be met. It would be incredibly transformative if the dominant parenting culture shifted its focus from the behavior of children to the behavior of adults, and its fascination with good behavior to an understanding of healthy child development. What would it be like to gauge the success of our disciplinary efforts *not* based on the child's behavior but, rather, on our own?

Children do not have the communication skills necessary to effectively communicate many of their needs to us, so nature has made sure children have other means by which to ensure big people understand what is required in any given moment. When infants cry, the caring adult knows that a diaper may need to be changed or a belly may need to be fed. When children are ill and whimpering in bed, the adult is compelled to swoop in and nurture them through the sickness. And when children are overwhelmed, unsettled, tired, "hangry" (hungry and angry), frustrated, disappointed, sad, mad, or any other variety of all-encompassing emotion, they are naturally equipped to let their big people know. Rather than being a conscious decision to push mommy's buttons, as they are often perceived to be, these loud, colorful, unpleasant, and otherwise interesting actions are really just children subconsciously doing what they *must* do to have their needs met by their big people. Behavior is simply a method of communication.

It is through this communication of needs that our children's absolute need of us—the big people—becomes so apparent, and explains why so often their behaviors are directed at, or occur in the presence of, their big people. Children depend on adults for the ultimate experience of being known and loved.[6] The science of child development has resolutely determined that this connection between big people and children is one of the most important, if not *the* most important, foundations of healthy child development. So much so that the United Nations listed as a key principle the child's right to grow up "in an atmosphere of happiness, love, and understanding."[7] As we consider what it means to raise a child in this kind of atmosphere, and we think about where we most need to apply this standard for today's child, my suggestion is that we consider how our approaches to disciplining children measure up against our children's primary need of contact, connection, and closeness with the big people in their lives.

The most common reasons parents request support in my practice are because of behavioral challenges, anxiety, depression, emotional upset about life transitions, and other things that are making a child's day-to-day life difficult (and, indeed, making the life of the child's caring adults difficult too). Of course, children facing these kinds of things in life communicate their related needs by "acting out"—or, in other words, through their behavior. When I talk with parents about the potential sources of their child's upset, I often steer the conversation around to discipline. At this point, many go on to list all the traditional approaches to discipline—such as time-outs, consequences, removal of privileges, reward programs, and targeted praise—they have been using to attempt to control their children. These attempts have not worked and never will. In fact, these approaches seem to cause an escalation in the behavioral challenges of the children being disciplined.

When we work together, I ask parents to imagine the world through their child's eyes. With the child's perspective firmly front and center, parents and other big people stop trying to change the behavior and instead begin to look at why it is occurring and what support must be put in place for the child's needs to be fully met. They begin to respond to their child informed by that understanding and by compassion, and they see real and lasting changes. When we acknowledge the true needs of children and set up a world in which those needs will be met—with imagination, patience, and compassion—we champion their healthy development. We also allow them to come to understand the norms of behavior that the world will require of them without ever requiring them to sacrifice their trust in, and connection with, us. I've seen it happen in my practice many times.

The capacity to exact a positive and enduring influence on a child's life is perhaps the greatest responsibility we will ever have. And yet the dominant parenting culture today has taken us very far away from understanding that our children's core need is their connection to *us*. Instead, it has walked us directly into approaches to discipline that are damaging to our children.[8] Let me tell you a personal story that illustrates how pervasive this idea of the "need" for *damaging* discipline is in parenting culture.

On a dreary autumn day when both of my boys had a school holiday, the rain was pouring down. Rather than going stir crazy at home, we decided to brave the chaos of an indoor play center near our house. I took several deep breaths to ready myself for the impending onslaught of activity, noise, and general insanity, and off we went. As soon as we arrived, it immediately became clear that indeed we were not the only family that had chosen this spot to survive a rainy day. Children were running everywhere, their exuberant shouts reverberating in the air. While I have always secretly endeavored to be that parent that can manage such a scene with a totally relaxed vibe—drinking my latte, chatting with other parents, keeping a quiet eye on my littles—on this particular day, in this particular setting, the vibe was anything but relaxed. I poked my head in and out of slide chutes and stairwells (hello chiropractor!), sometimes joining in and other times trying to pull back to be sure everyone was safely having fun.

And then it happened. I spotted my younger son, Maxwell, who was just 3 ½ years old, coming towards me full throttle, his cheeks bright red with exertion, his blond locks glued to his forehead with perspiration, and an expression on his sweet face that clearly communicated all was not well. He launched himself into my waiting arms, and, as I prepared to go into "calming mode," he wound up and plowed his dimpled little hand, now in a closed fist, square into my nose. Awesome. Even though my nose was throbbing and my eyes were tearing involuntarily, I realized that Maxwell had become very unsettled and needed a lot of care in that moment. So I increased my soothing efforts, and within a minute or 2 I felt his little body relaxing into my arms. The hurts, overwhelmed feelings, fatigue, or whatever it was that had caused the meltdown were slowly being taken care of by the comforting touch that I knew I could provide.

As I continued to calm Maxwell down, the crowd of parents around us suddenly fell silent and stared. I could almost hear their unspoken thoughts: "Are you really going to let him get away with that?" "That kid needs some discipline!" "Wow, look where airy-fairy parenting got that mom." "She should teach him a lesson." Still holding Maxwell and without making eye contact with any of the other parents, I found a chair to sink down into so he could be safely held in my cozy lap. And that is when "Perfect Mom," a woman I had never met before, shared some parenting advice with me. Her words, now etched into my memory, were: "You know, time-outs work pretty well."

Now, being a passionate person, especially about a) my children and b) my convictions about the needs of children in general, it was very difficult for me not to launch into a twelve-minute lecture on the developing brain of a young child; its need for connection to feel safe, secure, and regulated; and the role of comforting big people in helping a child to grow into the kind of adult who meshes beautifully with the world. Instead, I silently counted to ten and said simply, "Well, in our house we have decided to parent through connection and so time-outs are not something we do." That, Perfect Mom, is just how we roll, I thought to myself. Of course, she had no idea that my life's work has been to ensure that children's needs are deeply understood and compassionately met.

It was interesting to see how the brakes went on for Perfect Mom—you could read it in her face. She looked at me with an expression that seemed to say, "Uh-oh, she knows something I don't. What to do . . . ?" And then she said aloud to me, "Well, in our house we find we don't actually have to use time-outs because the threat of them is good enough." A couple of parents in the posse standing close by murmured their endorsement. And at that I smiled as pleasant a smile as I could muster as I began to gather up our things, transition Maxwell and his brother into "going-home mindsets," and decisively left the chaos of the indoor play center behind us.

The story doesn't end there. As I settled my boys into the car, knowing that Maxwell was calm, I smiled into his eyes. I told him kindly that I understood he had had a tricky time at the play center, but the next time things got tricky, he was to come to me for help and I would be counting on him to not use his hitting hands but to be gentle. He nodded his agreement. And that was that. It was not discussed again. I did not berate him in front of my husband at the family dinner table nor relive the moment again in any other way. And here is where the message really comes home. Two days later as I was settling Maxwell to sleep, unprompted he reached up to my face with his baby-soft hands. He placed one hand on each of my cheeks and said gently, "Mommy, I am sorry I hit you at the play place."

It occurs to me to wonder if all of the parents who watched the nose-punch scene and felt I responded inappropriately could ever have imagined this outcome. Could they have predicted that by responding to my upset child with compassion and empathy—by first regulating him and then inviting from him an intention to be gentle next time around—I was creating a way for the nose-punch moment to blossom into an unprompted and heartfelt apology? Could they have guessed that in appearing to "let him get away with it" I had actually gifted him a deep experience of what it is to be loved, taken care of, and *known?* Could they have fathomed that in refraining from "teaching him a lesson" while he was melting down in the chaos of the play center, I had allowed my child to learn exactly what he needed to learn that day? I would suggest that the answer to all of these questions for that group of parents on that rainy fall day—and indeed for most big people on most days—is a definite no.

Maxwell's "learning" came about because he experienced what it felt like to be cared for and understood. In experiencing this, he came one small step closer to becoming the settled and sorted grown adult I dream of him becoming: the kind of adult who is able to interact with the world in a manner that has him feeling happy and fulfilled and who will be a contributing member of society. The evidence of this experience didn't appear for a few days, but at the time of the upset I trusted that I had given him what he needed when he didn't have the words—only his explosive behavior—to express that he needed it.

There are two main reasons we big people seemed to have lost our clear understanding of the needs of children when it comes to disciplining them. First, we are immersed in a parenting "pop culture" in which we judge the appropriate reaction to a child's behavior based on the behavior itself rather than the needs and feelings of the child. That is, our dominant parenting pop culture is one that assigns value only to what is seen on the outside—behavior—rather than to what is occurring on the inside. Second, at the same time, we are having to make decisions and complete tasks more quickly than ever before. Life has never been so fast-paced! As parents and other big people hurry around dealing with the pressures of work and extracurricular activities and school and life, we have fallen victim to a quick-fix mentality. We need a "solution" now, here, immediately! We need quiet *now*, peace *now*, cooperation *now!* As a result, we have lost sight of what is essential to the growing child. In our modern lives, there is no time to consider the deep-seated needs of a child and cultivate the adaptability and resilience that we know will eventually lead to emotional settling, and in turn, to calmer behavior.

I have a message for the parenting pop culture of today and the high-pressured world around us. The traditional approach to discipline that understands challenging behavior as something that must be stopped, no matter what, simply does not work. There is a better way. From the outside, it may look messier. It may require some delayed gratification. And it may force us to swim upstream at times, suffering the scorn of others around us. But it takes the very best that the science of child development has to offer and invites us to implement it with nurturing care. It is wonderfully empowering to know that as big people we are perfectly positioned to be the epicenter of a positive shift for all of our children. And it is wonderfully freeing to know that in fully embracing the natural order of child development we can truly meet the needs of our children, allowing them to grow up in the best possible way. Every single big person has the potential to be this support for the children in our care. And if every one of us who takes on the task of growing up children were to focus on understanding children's needs and our central role in meeting those needs, the profound positive impact on whole generations would be mind-boggling!

This book will show you why and how to move from the rushed, reflexive parenting pop culture that is dominant today to create a settled and healthy world in which kids can experience connection with their big people. The book is divided into two main sections that will allow you to really integrate science with practice. The guiding mantra throughout is See It, Feel It, Be It! Core to the embodiment of this mantra is the idea that there is no such thing as a guaranteed strategy for making discipline work, there is no magic set of steps, and there is no fixed solution for any given situation. Rather, in coming to deeply understand the needs of children (SEE it) and in turn feeling compassion for your children in the moments when those needs present behaviorally or otherwise (FEEL it), you will be instinctively compelled to respond in a manner that is magically suited to the moment and your children's needs (BE it).

Part I presents a clear understanding of what discipline is... and what it is not. You'll learn how a child's brain grows and why that matters to how we as big people correct, teach, and comfort them. We examine common situations in which children act out and look behind the obvious to what is really going on inside the child's mind and heart, and what is really going on within the big person–child connection. I'll show you how some discipline tactics damage and how a nurturing approach centered on relationship can both give children what they need and get you what you want.

Real change doesn't happen overnight, and there will be times when you will need to keep the faith that your decision to parent through connection is what your child truly needs, especially when it comes to discipline. You'll have to be bigger, wiser, and stronger—not to mention more patient—than your child, but the good news is that you have a mature brain and the whole of Part II to help you. I give you countless suggestions about how to respond both in those crucial moments of meltdown and outside of them, when you can focus on building that best possible world for your child.

My overarching goal is to awaken within you an intuitive heart, which is the key to developing an understanding of your child's needs. With that understanding, you will be confident of your ability to meet those needs in the acute moments and in more peaceful times too, by creating a developmentally informed world for your child that prevents upset where possible and avoids isolation at all costs. I know there are days when putting one foot in front of another and breathing in and out is difficult: growing up a child is really hard work. I know it is sometimes hard to see your way through to the other side of a challenge when you are buried deep within it. It is for this reason that I have taken extra care in Part II to provide you with tangible, doable examples of the See It, Feel It, Be It mantra in action. If at first you can't see it or feel it, then follow the tips in chapter 7 to just start *being* it. Put another way, if you are feeling lost but you urgently need an answer about how to respond to your child's behaviors—say, a tricky time getting out of the house in the mornings (pages 157, 158, and 159), a hard time at bedtime (pages 188, 189, and 190), or a moment that has you ready to throw in the towel (pages 190, 191, and 192)—I give you some ideas about what to do so you can "fake it" until you "make it."

It is my hope that as you read this book, you will find the influence imposed upon you by the dominant parenting pop culture melting away. In place of this blurry allegiance to peer pressure and social norms, you will sense your innate ability to respond to your child's behavior come alive in a manner that nature intended and that science supports. Discipline that focuses only on extinguishing challenging behaviors can damage children. But thoughtful approaches that seek to understand the underlying reasons for behavior and address these compassionately, embraced by caring big people, champions children, paving the way for brilliant outcomes. May you find in the pages of this book inspiration to be that kind of a big person. And as you do, know that your children are lucky to have you.

I

CONNECTION MAKES
THE WORLD GO 'ROUND
& GROWS BRAINS

WHAT DISCIPLINE IS & IS NOT

Everyone has an opinion about discipline. Experts weigh in on the subject from every angle, and parents often say they feel totally lost in knowing what works and what doesn't, what they are supposed to be doing and not doing. Typically by the time their children reach their second birthday, parents are consumed by the subject of discipline. They wonder, am I going to mess my child up for life? Is everyone around me going to judge my parenting? Is my child going to be able to survive in a kindergarten classroom? Am I being too tough? Am I being too soft? Does she know I love her? Will he still love me? Is this going to work? Am I slowly wrecking her? If it doesn't feel right, should I still do it? These kinds of questions are very natural for caring big people to have. To give you answers to some of these questions and put you at ease with others of them, I will walk you through the basic science of child development and how you can translate this knowledge into action for your child.

WHAT IS DISCIPLINE?

When we feel overwhelmed by not really knowing how to approach discipline, big people often turn to the Internet and books to try to figure it out. The trouble is that rather than answering questions, the information overload from all of these many sources often creates even more questions. And most of these sources offer a version of *how* to discipline, with very little discussion about *why*. My belief is that there is no getting to the *how* if we have not first figured out *why*. And to figure out why, we really need to ask a simple question: what is discipline?

Many times when I ask this question at workshops, in support sessions, or onsite at community daycares, schools, and other places, the answers I get have something to do with preparing children for the realities of the world. A lot of us believe that our children are going to have to conform to the standards, regulations, expectations, and rules of the world around them sooner or later, so we might as well pave the way by firmly applying said standards, regulations, expectations, and rules right away. If we don't, we reason, how will they ever keep friends? How will they ever succeed at school? How will they ever hold down a job? The thinking behind such a response is that children need to learn to walk within the lines and do things as the world expects.

While I don't disagree that things may become quite challenging for a child who cannot keep her unkind thoughts to herself, who cannot get moving on a task or chore that has to be completed, or who cannot be relatively pleasant to the people around her, I have some trouble with the logic that extending adult realities to a child's world is actually going to create the desired outcomes. That is, many big people assume that because their children will have to take it on the chin, suck it up, and carry on when they become adults, subjecting children to those harsh realities in childhood will give them lots of time to prepare for adulthood. Unfortunately, developmental science does not support this theory.

Instead, as the term "developmental" alludes to, growing up involves a progression through many different levels of capacity and maturity. Children are not just smaller versions of adults.

Developmentally, children are very different from big people. The frontal and prefrontal cortex in their brains are comparatively immature, and as a result, children have a lesser capacity for self-control. Put another way, children are naturally impulsive until their brains develop enough to allow them to exercise self-control. In studies conducted in the 1960s and '70s, the famous Stanford marshmallow experiment showed this correlation between self-control and age. Young children were seated in an empty room at a table that had a marshmallow on it. They were told they could eat that marshmallow if they wanted, but if they waited fifteen minutes, they would be allowed to eat 2 marshmallows. The results showed that the older the child, the more likely it was that she would wait and reap the rewards of the second marshmallow. Or in other words, self-control comes with *development* and is strengthened over time and with experience. That is, adults are always going to be better at self-control than children because they are older.

If the frontal and prefrontal cortex are the areas of the brain most strongly implicated in the ability to maintain self-control, and these areas of the brain are the last to mature for the growing child, then it makes sense that children are naturally not going to have a lot of self-control.[1] So until nature has actually grown for them the neural infrastructure needed to support self-control, it really does not make sense that we ask children to conform to the standards, regulations, expectations, and rules of the world. They simply *cannot*—as opposed to *will not*—follow through on much of what big people might demand from them in terms of self-control.

And yet, if we relentlessly focus on "preparing children for the realities of the adult world" by insisting they exert "self-control" in a variety of situations at very young ages, we are driven to impose sanctions like consequences and time-outs, and almost desperately concoct strategies like reward charts so that our children behave "appropriately." In essence, we are using these sanctions and concoctions as disciplinary measures to have children mimic self-control. The unfortunate reality is that a child's brain can be tricked into conformity—but *not* into self-control. It is possible to create a behavioral façade of self-control by playing upon the social-emotional needs of the child. Children need an emotional connection with their special big people, and by tying this social-emotional need to discipline, as a reward or punishment for behavior that mimics self-control, we can trick a child's brain and manipulate the resulting behavior. It is exactly at this juncture that we sacrifice the needs of our child in the name of good behavior, and it is exactly here that discipline becomes damaging.

☛ Discipline is not self-control

As a social species, children are born into this world looking for us. In the words of Dr. Jeree Pawl, a child development specialist, "Everything that we know about [children] leads to the conclusion that they seek human connection, not only to survive but for its own sake. They are born looking for us. Given a choice of what to look at in their first hours, it is always the human face they choose."[2] Children have an intuitive sense of their need for us that is evident to any observer from the very first moments of life.

Indeed, contemporary research in the field of child development has consistently gifted us the understanding that a child's emotional and physical connection to her special big people is absolutely essential to survival and development.[3] And it is this absolute reliance on, and need for, connection that our parenting pop culture has co-opted in the name of discipline and "self-control" for children. Our hyperfocus on discipline has twisted the notion of self-control together with a child's core need for connection, with the result that discipline means using a child's need for connection to essentially scare her into "self-control" (good behavior). While this approach to discipline may appear to yield the desired behavior, it does so in the most damaging of ways.

If a child holds as his most essential need *connectedness* in physical and emotional ways to his special big person, then this child's brain will put everything on hold until that connection is realized. Consider the situation where a 4-year-old is playing with another child and having difficulty sharing a toy. To prevent him from stealing the coveted toy away from the other child, the adults around this child might say, "We must share with our friend," and then put a limit on each child's time playing with the toy. However, these attempts at structuring "self-control" are inevitably going to fail. The child waiting for his turn will not be able to resist diving in for a grab, push, and dash with the toy. After all, this child's brain may not yet be mature enough to allow self-control in this situation.

A big person who is well schooled in our dominant parenting pop culture will see this behavior as a departure from the dictated social norms and rules and feel compelled to "teach" the child a "lesson" so that the child will do better next time and, ultimately, be more prepared for the realities of the world. This adult might tell the child to retreat to a "thinking chair" until he is feeling more calm, and when he is ready to play nicely he will be welcome to come back and play. If you were to watch this scene unfold, the child might initially cry and resist placement on the thinking chair, maybe even get angry. Eventually, if forced to stay on the thinking chair, the child would sooner or later appear to have "calmed." The adults would welcome him back to the play situation, where the child would seem to be more compliant in sharing. Lesson learned and mission accomplished by way of an aptly applied discipline strategy, right? Wrong.

If you were to continue to simply look at the situation as a matter of behavior—that is, with a focus on the idea that the child must "learn" to share the toy—you might be convinced that the child had indeed learned an important lesson and changed his behavior. The problem is, we know from the science of child development that the child very likely is not capable of maintaining self-control and, as a result, cannot share the toy. We also know that the child's connection to his big people is his most important need. Keeping these two facts in mind, let's look at the situation again within our developmental framework. When made to sit on the thinking chair, the child likely experienced both an emotional disconnect from his big person (who may have been talking in a stern voice, looking unhappy, or even voicing discontent directly) as well as a physical disconnect from his big person (who was not sitting with him). As this child's need for connectedness will trump all other needs until it is addressed, his neural pathways will direct him to do just about anything to right the perceived wrong and re-establish the connection with his big person. So the tears in the thinking chair cease and reaching to steal the toy stops, and the child appears to have been successfully brought back into line. But *at what cost?*

The cost is that the child's need for connectedness has been used as a bargaining chip. What has the child really learned? He has not "learned" anything, but he has "experienced" something significant. He has been sent a message that has landed deep within his developing sense of self. And this message is that his foundational need for connection is not being unconditionally met, but rather it is contingent upon "good behavior." He has internalized this message without any whiff of understanding. This is why he has not "learned" anything. Instead, the impact of the disciplinary response has occurred automatically as his brain has mechanistically (without conscious thought) responded to his developmental needs and effected an outcome that will shape his future behavior. This is the damage that has been done.

☛ *Discipline is a way of being that supports connection*
To avoid falling into the trap of playing a child's needs against him in the name of "good behavior," and further, to avoid conflating damaging

discipline with "good behavior" and "self-control," let us consider the original question. What is discipline? If we think about what every parent and big person dreams of for their children, it is usually that they will grow up into adults who are relatively happy, settled, and contributing members of society, and who act with respect, patience, a sense of ethics, and generosity towards other people. What does it take to grow up a child so that such outcomes can be realized? Ultimately, the thoughts and actions of happy, settled, contributing members of society result from neurons speaking to other neurons in a very specific kind of way. So to grow up children who are going to be okay as adults, we are hoping to lovingly sculpt for them a brain that is going to work in accomplishing this aim.

The next chapter will address more thoroughly the science of exactly how this happens, but the heart of it is that it involves a lot of connection, compassion, and nurturance from big people. As adults, our goal then becomes to gift our children as many opportunities as possible, especially and most importantly in behaviorally challenging moments, to absolutely affirm their safety and place in the world through an unconditional connection to us.

So what is discipline? Instead of seeing it as a series of prescribed actions, think of discipline as *a way of being* that allows us to see an abundant supply of opportunities to connect with our children in ways that truly resonate with their developmental needs. It is in discipline that we have a wonderful entry point into really punctuating safety—physically and emotionally—as a defining feature of a child's world. It is in discipline that we mold neural pathways that promote regulation and, eventually, self-control. And it is in discipline that we take significant leaps towards promoting the development of positive self-concept and self-confidence. Discipline is that loosely defined but broadly applied cluster of ideas, interpretations, and feelings—and flowing from all of that, subsequent actions—that allow us to guide our children through their most formative years to emerge as healthy, whole beings who can intersect with their world in meaningful ways. Discipline is not something that you *do* so much as it is something that you *be*. Paradoxically, discipline is actually about the behaviors of big people rather than those of children.

If discipline is about creating a sense of safety, regulation, and confidence, then we should be committed to 2 things. First, to ensuring a safe emotional and physical environment that respects a child's greatest need—the need for connection to us. Second, to acting with a full understanding of how a child's experiences with connection impact brain development. Unfortunately, big people rarely think of discipline this way. Therefore, instead of experiencing discipline in a safe and connected manner, our children are often manipulated into conforming to "good" behavior in adults' mistaken belief that this will lead to "success" in life. In the ultimate quest for well-behaved children—stoked by this desire for success—we sell our children out to the façade of conformity proffered by "good" behavior at any cost. How did we become convinced that this was the way to go? A look at our historical perspectives about who children are helps to answer that question.

HISTORICAL PERSPECTIVES & CONTEMPORARY BIASES

Through the ages, children have been viewed through a variety of lenses, each of which led to a different approach to childrearing and application of "discipline." Three dominant philosophical views deserve mention as we consider the most influential of these lenses.[4]

In the Middle Ages and into the early 1600s, children were often thought to have been born inherently evil, a philosophy typically referred to as the *original sin* view of the child. Through this perspective, a child's most desperate need was salvation, and it was the responsibility of the adults around a child to purge her of evil inclinations, rid her of sin, and fill her with all that is pure and holy. There was no room for developmental perspectives and growth continuums within such a harsh theoretical stance. Rather, children were treated as tiny adults, even often dressed as tiny adults, and most definitely harshly punished as tiny adults.

By the late 1600s, the predominant thinking about children had changed. Children's brains were thought of as a blank slate, a *tabula rasa*, and adults were responsible for putting forward the energy and resources to fill up their child's brain with the traits, values, and thoughts consistent with what they wanted their child to become in adulthood. Behaviorist John B. Watson, bolstered by this tabula rasa view, famously stated: "Give me a dozen healthy infants, well-formed, and my own specified world to bring them up in and I'll guarantee to take any one at random and train him to become any type of specialist I might select—doctor, lawyer, artist, merchant-chief, and, yes, even beggar-man and thief, regardless of his talents, penchants, tendencies, abilities, vocations, and race of his ancestors."[5]

In both the original sin and tabula rasa perspectives, key threads of bias are woven throughout. First, there is very little room for the child to be a unique person. A child's individual temperament, naturally occurring interests, gifted abilities, or other innate attributes simply have no place. Second, development is not viewed as a continuum—a child just is and has to be. There is no chance to morph and change and emerge and grow in a manner that is aligned with physical and emotional development. Third, the focus is on adults putting something into the child or getting something out of the child, but very little emphasis is placed on cultivating the child's own growth and innate ability to be, produce, and feel.

Though few big people today would openly espouse the original sin or tabula rasa perspectives, I guarantee that if you were to watch parents and their antsy children standing in line at any grocery or department store you would see all sorts of remnants of these parenting philosophies in the musings of the other adults in the lineup. As the children fidget, fight, run around, and bump into other people and their carts, you would likely hear customers echoing (or at least thinking) the same kinds of things parents said on the day Maxwell landed his punch on my nose, "Are you really going to let him get away with that?" or "A little bit of discipline might help!" or "You should teach that little brat a lesson!" Reinterpreted more harshly, these comments might be translated as "Force more conformity upon him!" and "Squash those explosive instincts in him!" and "Get the rotten bits out of him!" That is, those musings are all informed by the biases that thousands of years of parenting philosophies have passed down through the generations and deposited in our collective psyche.

In the 1700s, another parenting philosophy called the *innate goodness* view came into favor. Very different in flavor to the previous two, this perspective presented the idea that children are actually born innately good. The responsibility of the parent in this case is to release the child into the proverbial flowery meadows and watch her grow, with as little parental interference as possible. And while this view does not provoke the same recoiling horror as the original sin view might, it nevertheless causes most of us today to shake our heads in disagreement. We know that children require boundaries and expectations to feel safe and sorted in this crazy world we call home. And yet the biases of the innate goodness view also live on, as we quietly fret about whether we are doing the right things. Perhaps we would do better to leave well enough alone? Maybe our reaction was too harsh, too demanding, too involved, too much? At an extreme, this bias might lead to permissive parenting, in which parents become so frightened of squashing their child's spirit that they forget their role as big people is needed to lead and define and sculpt.

In the present day, most of us at least pay lip service to understanding childhood as a very important, unique period of life. We champion childhood with such mantras as "the early years last forever" and as a society we have dedicated whole systems to protect, educate, and ensure the health of children. The intent of these systems is to allow us to cherish the impact of a child's experiences as ultimately important to their growth and development. And yet the historical philosophies of parenting and childrearing—although antiquated and outdated—live on in those insidious biases and continue to stretch their long fingers into our present approaches to discipline. Think about phrases like "tough love" and "spare the rod, spoil the child" and "we should not do for a child that which they can and should do for themselves," which persist in influencing parenting even today. None of these biases champion the scientifically documented universal need of the child—connection—and none of these biases champion the developmental perspective that childhood is a unique and exceptional period in life, not just an immature form of adulthood.

A CONTEMPORARY PERSPECTIVE: DELIGHTFUL CHAOS

When we discipline by connection, we are creating infinite opportunities to absolutely do right by our children, but there are many things we should not do. Supreme amongst these is to use discipline as a way of imposing order and control on what is meant to be the delightful chaos of childhood. That is, in getting bogged down with wanting to limit "misbehavior," we pass up opportunities to embrace development.

A few years back, I was piecing together a presentation for early childhood professionals and I came across a website extolling the benefits of a system of discipline based around presenting consequences for children. Although the exact quote escapes me, it was something like " ... because as you well know, the higher goal of parenting is to find your child behaving well and reinforce that." Ask yourself if this really is your higher goal? Is finding your children behaving "well," and consistently reinforcing that, the true pathway to growing them towards all they were intended to be? Is a child who is not behaving "well" a "bad" child? Or, in the context of understanding behavior as a child's way of communicating an unmet need, should we simply embrace its wild and wonderful world as a healthy and normal part of development?

The problem with approaches that champion "good" behavior and use this as a proxy for "success" in adulthood is that they have lost sight of the true nature of childhood, children's needs, and their best path to development. Children are not just immature adults. They are children! They have all sorts of stretching and growing to do. There will be stops and starts. There will be mountains and valleys. And to be very clear, in the most ideal circumstances, the end product is likely to—and indeed, should—look very, very different from its incarnations along the way. The intense, sensitive, and at times explosive child who is consistently reacted to with calm, nurturing, understanding, safe, and firm boundaries can morph in adulthood into an empathetic, introspective, driven human being. The adults that our children will become are going to be so different from the processes and experiences that will shape them along the way. Nobody ever said that childhood was going to be neat and tidy and pretty and calm. (Nobody worth listening to anyway.) In fact, childhood that is going well is going to be anything but! Your children may cry, they may melt down, they may hit, they may lash out. But all of these things are *supposed* to be part of the journey.

A friend of mine who was a physics major once told me that people enjoy the sound of a babbling brook, and often find it very peaceful and relaxing because the movement of the water up and down and over and around all of the stones results in a cacophony of sound waves that essentially cancel each other out. That is, it is the friction of the water getting bashed all about that makes the brook peaceful. I like to think of the developmental journey that is childhood, especially in discussing the challenging behaviors our children can have, as this babbling brook. There will be moments when our efforts to grow up our children all seem to be falling apart and other moments when these efforts appear to be coming together beautifully. You may have stretches when you feel like you have gotten nowhere, and other times when you feel like you are leaps and bounds ahead. And there may be times when you look at your child's behavior and are completely unable to see the virtues behind it. Experienced holistically, and with the ultimate respect for child development and the science inherent to it, this delightful chaos is the peaceful, babbling brook that we call childhood. It is *meant* to be a cacophony of experiences that weave together to create the most beautiful, happy, adaptable human being we can imagine.

Our job as adults is to cherish this chaos. Rather than focusing on creating order and quiet, focus instead on making room for childhood to unfold. Find ways to let yourself relax. Ignore the standards of the world around you and, instead, zero in on what your children need. What they need is you. They need your compassion. They need your presence. They need your understanding. They need you to feel them. They need you to protect them. This does not mean you have to be perfect every day. All it takes is for you to be "good enough" for your child's brain to grow and develop as nature intended. In working *with* the science of child development and responding to the foundational need of our children for connection, we fulfill our responsibility as adults not only in how we approach discipline but in all aspects of a child's world. Simply by continually ensuring our children's connection with us, we gift them the opportunity to become all that they can be. In the "See It, Feel It, Be It" call to action of this book, this is the SEE it part. We need to get inside the minds of our children and look out at the world through their eyes. We need to see the world the way they see it, so we can embrace childhood for what it really is, and in so doing, embrace our role in this for our children. When you can really and truly look out at the world through the eyes of your child, and really and truly feel deep inside your intuitive big person's heart the needs and hopes and wants of your child, you will have everything required to *be* for your child exactly what science and nature demand of you. This is all that it takes to see, feel, and be.

THE SCIENCE & HEART OF CONNECTION

When children need something, they let us know. Day in and day out as children experience needs, the attachment system that controls their drive to connect with their big people becomes activated, and they behave in connection-seeking ways that create opportunities for big people to respond and help children's brains grow in the best possible way. A child's attachment system will activate in 1 of 3 situations—when a child is ill, physically hurt, or emotionally upset—in order to prompt the child to seek out connection and have their precipitating need met. It is nature's way of ensuring that children are responded to in developmentally safe ways.

Big people are generally quite good at seeing the upset in a child who is ill and feeling compassionately moved to care for the child in that moment. How often have you found yourself cleaning up after a child that has vomited in her bed? It's 2 a.m. and you are exhausted and wanting desperately to sleep, but in that moment you will yearn to take care of your child. You will strip beds and tumble puked-on sheets into the laundry. You will remake the bed, shower or bathe your child, and ensure she is safely settled back into a comfortable, cozy fresh bed before you address your own needs of sleep and restoration.

It also appears that big people are fairly adept at responding to the needs of a child who has physically hurt himself. How many times have you been at a playground and seen a child fall? All the big people immediately gasp and start to move towards the child to ensure he is taken care of. Nobody would dream of leaving the poor little guy in the middle of the playground, crying out from his injury. Of course, we all rush in and tend to him without reservation.

While we have illness and physical injury in the bag, our responses to a child who is activated emotionally seem often to be decidedly different. How do we know when children are emotionally upset? In infants, the seeking behaviors of an activated attachment system (those behaviors that ensure a child's need is met with connection) typically involve crying. Most big people feel compassion for crying infants and respond accordingly with soothing and physical connection. As children get a little bit older, the seeking behaviors take on a different tone. The crying of the infant might turn into the howls of the toddler. Those howls might become hits and kicks by age 3. Full meltdowns often happen by this age as well. At ages 5 and 6, verbal aggression, such as name calling, may have become part of the package. These behaviors then morph to become the door slamming of the 8-year-old, the stonewalling of the 11-year-old, and the freezing out of the 14-year-old. All of these responses—whether the infant's crying, the toddler's howling, the ill child's whimpering, the hurt child's sobbing, or the upset preteen's deafening silence—originate in exactly the same way in the brain. And the attachment activation system is the same, whether the cause was throwing up, falling in the playground, or wanting a toy the child cannot have. And yet, most of us don't recognize that. It is rare in the dominant parenting pop culture to find experts and methods that encourage us to see the behavior of an emotionally upset, angry, frustrated, or just downright yelly-shouty child and feel compassionately moved to rush in and soothe the activated system behind that behavior... or rather "misbehavior." Why?

The reason harkens back to many of the factors discussed in chapter 1. We have thousands of years of bias that have crept into our subconscious views about children. And our generation of parents is stressed out, short on time, and overwhelmed by the expectations life has placed both on us and on our children. At the same time we have never before been so isolated in our parenting journeys, often finding ourselves without the benefit of connected extended families and communities to support us along the way. These conditions have collided to create a popular approach to discipline that does not meet the needs of children, and, in fact, is harmful to their developing brains and their burgeoning sense of self. In our stressed, overwhelmed state we need their "bad" behavior to stop, and stop now! We don't have time to sort through this situation thoughtfully. And if we dare to take the time, we suffer the scorn of all those around us who think we need to act faster to take care of the "problem" that is our child's behavior.

THE DISCONNECT

When we discipline our children, we often fall prey to the temptation to act quickly, stop the behavior, and avoid the judgment of others. We use strategies like time-outs, consequences, removal of privileges, and reward charts to get our children to fall into line. Each of these strategies has at its core "the disconnect." That is, they play on the child's most essential need, which is connection to us, and put it on the line to secure the child's "good behavior." In essence, the child's need for us becomes a ploy we use against them to have them behave, a ploy concocted to ensure good behavior. The child gets access to us if behaving well but is disconnected if not behaving well. And in a desperate effort to restore the connection, the child begins to behave. It is the cost of this "good" behavior that is the primary concern. Why would we ever put into play the one thing that is most essential to a child's well-being? How is it possible that we consider "good" behavior more valuable than a brain that functions in a healthy way, that will serve our children well in adulthood, and that provides them the chance to actualize into settled, happy, contributing members of society?

To meet the child's most foundational need for connectedness in any kind of moment when that need might be activated, we must find ways to understand our responses to behavior through the lens of connection. We need to know how to *be* in the moment, as our children's meltdowns happen and as their yelly-shouties fly about. We need to find ways to scoop our children up and protect them from emotional damage, just as we would save them from physical peril. We need to find ways to connect with their brains and their hearts so we can competently settle them, and in the process, grow for them a brain capable of defeating stress and remaining regulated.

Regulation is about being able to calm oneself down and construct and maintain a healthy view of reality and flexible emotions. Children need the help of big people to regulate, and if they are well supported in this process when they are young, they will develop the capacity to become increasingly capable of regulating on their own by adulthood. Children cannot be forced into a regulated state. They must experience years and years of adults responding calmly and compassionately to upsets to develop the neural infrastructure necessary to truly self-regulate. A person who can self-regulate is a genuinely mature and independent being, but this state of true independence only arises from the enduring experience of deep dependence. And the key, once again, is in connection.

THE CONNECTION AT FIRST SIGHT

A child is born looking for us.[1] Newborn babies will instinctively seek out our eyes as they squeak open their own eyes for those first bleary glances around the world they have arrived in. And when they do find our eyes, they will lock on to them and hold that gaze. An adult on the receiving end of such a gaze knows the profound power in that exchange. As the newborn baby stares with those sweet, unblinking eyes, it feels as though that baby reaches in and grabs a hold of our heart, sealing a bond for life. We are absolutely and completely in love with them. As a result of their stare, we would do anything for them. Powerful!

In fact, neuroscience supports what has happened in those moments. Specifically, during the birth process and in the moments following, and then again in other moments of intense connection, our adult brain is awash in the neurotransmitter oxytocin,[2] the "love" chemical known for its intense bonding properties around connectedness and relationships. Scientists have also found that even beyond the bonding experience of oxytocin-fueled moments, a baby's fetal cells actually migrate across the placenta and land themselves in various places in a mother's body, including in her brain. These fetal cells are thought to act very much like stem cells, which help to protect a mother's health. Thus, the profound interconnectivity we have with our children is not just emotional; we are physically bonded to them through neurotransmitters and cells.[3] The message here is that connection is foundational to how we exist and are meant to conduct ourselves with our children.

THE PHYSICAL & EMOTIONAL CONNECTION

In the 1930s psychologist John Bowlby began his life's work of understanding the significance of the relationship between a child and a parent. Today, Bowlby is often referenced as the "Father of Attachment" for having brought to light the concept of "attachment" and especially the importance of a physical and emotional connection between children and their big people as part of a child's healthy development. Using a research paradigm called the Strange Situation in which a child endures a series of separations and reunions with a special big person, Bowlby observed the types of behaviors the child presented. Bowlby used these observations to disentangle the kinds of relationships that little people can have with their big people. He and his colleagues also looked at how the nature of those relationships have significant impacts on the health · and well-being of the child, both emotionally and physically, and in the short and long term.[4] Their results ignited a firestorm of research.

Whereas Bowlby's laboratory paradigm relied on physical separations to underscore the importance of *relationship* for the developing child, psychologist Dr. Edward Tronick created a laboratory paradigm that focused on the importance of *emotional connectedness* between children and their big people. In a paradigm called the Still Face, Dr. Tronick had parents engage in typical, playful, face-to-face interactions with their children and then instructed them to stop engaging with their child and put on the "still face" that showed no emotion. The parent and child continued to be face to face, but the emotional connection between them was halted by the still face. He demonstrated resoundingly that this experience is extremely stressful for children to endure. Very young children will often lose control of their bodily functions (excessive drooling, tonguing, vomiting) and posture due to the brain-based disregulation they experience in the face of the disconnect—even though it only lasts for 2 minutes. Older children will also become distraught in the face of the disconnect, sometimes crying and other times becoming aggressive towards the parent—doing *anything* to get the parent to re-engage. Thus, Tronick highlighted a child's essential need for connection to big people as not just a physical closeness, but more than that, as an emotional closeness that the child senses and feels.

The work of Bowlby, Tronick, and many other child development researchers since them has demonstrated irrefutably that children need strong, safe, and enduring emotional and physical connections with their big people in order to grow up optimally and become all that they were meant to become.

THE FEAR OF DISCONNECTION

Given that a child's connection with a big person is so foundational to the child's development, it is perhaps not surprising that, universally, a child's greatest fear is loss of connectedness with the big person or people of most significance. Regardless of the time, place, culture, and race, the darkest, deepest, and most utterly terrifying fear of every child everywhere is, and has always been, the possibility of losing us. This fear of losing that special connection is not just expressed emotionally, but also physically. Important brain processes in a developing child are driven by *how* that child has been cared for. The stress response center of the brain (the Hypothalamic-Pituitary-Adrenal (HPA) axis) is the epicenter of the interaction between caregiving and neural wiring.[5] Essentially, the stress response center fires up whenever a child's attachment system is activated—that is, when a child is emotionally upset, physically hurt, or ill. As the HPA axis engages, the child will instinctively initiate connection-seeking behaviors that will compel her to seek contact with her special big person. These might include crying and clinging but also "behaviors" intended to secure our attention so that we can meet our child's needs. As we respond with compassionate, nurturing care, the child's stress response center starts to become calmed.

This act of calming is the key component of healthy child development. One of the basic principles of neuroscience is that "neurons that fire together wire together."[6] Thus, as children have repeated experiences of being stressed and then being calmed by their big people through nurturing care, they grow stress response centers in their brains that are increasingly capable of "self-regulation," or calming. In essence, in having their big people externally regulate them and swoop in to calm down their activated stress center through connection, children are able to grow brains with the right kind of neurological wiring that allows self-regulation to be possible. This is why children do not "learn" to calm or self-regulate. Children *become capable of* calming and self-regulation through consistent experiences of having been calmed by their caring adults. These calming experiences physically transform the brain's stress response center and pave the way neurologically for the capacity of self-regulation.

For children who do not receive consistent, nurturing care, the outcome is very different. If a child too often experiences a fired-up stress response system and does not, in turn, experience the care of a nurturing special big person, this child's stress response system becomes very good at being fired up, but not so good at calming down. When a special big person is not available to them often enough to make sure the calm-down neurons fire, the child cannot wire this response and therefore does not develop the capacity to do it. This child develops a brain that is very good at being stressed but not able to calm down.

From an evolutionary perspective, being adept at being stressed makes good sense. In an environment without a lot of safety, an active stress response center would keep you very vigilant, on guard, and never too settled, all of which would be more likely to ensure your survival. So in a remarkably adaptive way, the brain of a child who is not consistently cared for and responded to in nurturing ways by a special big person will flex to the world around it and propel the child into a hyperaroused state if it appears this is what is needed for that child to survive. If the system stays aroused, the child will continue to escalate his behaviors in order to communicate to those around him that his needs have not been met. And if the child's system stays perpetually aroused, his connection-seeking behaviors will be everpresent. Typically, the big people in this child's life will become angry and/or annoyed as a result of the child's continuing connection-seeking behaviors. The fallout from the adult reactions then perpetuates the child's stressed state and reinforces it; in essence, the child needs to be alert so he becomes better equipped to see the fallout coming and can try to get out of the way in time.

THE POWER OF CARE

Indeed, these patterns of stress and behavior have been measured and observed repeatedly in populations of vulnerable children. Children who have been institutionalized early in life, and in those environments experienced neglectful care, go on to have very sensitive stress response systems that can fire up even when no obvious threat is present.[7] If these children are subsequently placed in a loving adoptive home, their initial response to even very slight, relatively benign stressors (such as a change in schedule, for example) is very strong. Their brains are commanding the release of high levels of cortisol (stress hormone) into their systems to ready them for whatever reactive or protective action might be required. However, and remarkably, as these children are exposed to consistent and contingent nurturing care from a special big person— that is, almost every time they express a need, an adult is there to care for and meet their need—their cortisol response patterns change. Over time, children who were once hyperreactive in responding to stress develop a more settled stress response system that can even approximate the system of children who did not suffer the early maltreatment.[8]

It is in this remarkable change that we understand *how* we big people can climb into the brain of a child and grow it up in the best possible way. We do this by caring for them. In fact, while we have never before had such significant access to the inner workings of the brain, we have yet to find any other way into a child's brain. Connecting with our children, caring for them, interacting with them, and absolutely ensuring they sense our presence—both emotionally and physically—is the only way to reach our caring hands into the emotional core of a child's brain and affect how it grows.

It is important to note that this powerful effect of care is possible only with a caregiver with whom the child has developed a trusting relationship. If the child were to receive the same kind of consistent care but from a different person every day, she would not experience the same calming effect that promotes the capacity for eventual self-regulation. This is because, over time, children develop "scripts," or internal stories, about how caregiving works. These scripts allow them to form expectations about how a big person might be expected to respond to their needs.[9] In an ideal situation, that script may be: "My big person loves me no matter what. When I am upset, my big person takes care of me. My big person will never leave me." A less-ideal script might be: "My big person might respond to my need but might not—I just have to wait and see. My big person is sometimes here for me but sometimes is not. My big person might leave me." By the time a child has reached 4 months of age, these scripts already exist (although these stories can be "rewritten" at any age) and he is very aware of which big people can be counted on and which cannot. Those scripts become part and parcel of the wiring in the stress response center of the brain.

The more that children experience caregiving in reaction to their needs, the more their scripts about caregiving with their special big people (e.g., their parents) can begin to extend to other big people. It is in this way that teachers, childcare providers, aunties, uncles, grandmas, grandpas, neighbors, therapists, and other people are granted entrée into the privileged role and extraordinary responsibility of growing up a child. This is the manner in which many members of the proverbial village come to grow up the child.

The nature of the relationship children have with their big people quite literally forms the foundation of the brain, including the HPA axis that controls the stress response system. Since brains mature from the bottom up, with all other layers of the brain resting upon this essential foundation,[10] this core is early on most actively the target of development. Once this central core has developed gradually over the first years of life, our outer "thinking" layers of the brain start to more actively mature. However, it is this emotional core that drives our attachment system and need for connection, survival responses, and other basic functions, whereas the outer layers allow us to become increasingly capable of problem solving, self-control, and other higher cognitive functions. And just as a building will be unstable if built upon a shaky foundation, so too will a brain struggle with subsequent development if built upon a highly reactive core. A brain that has benefited from consistent, nurturing caregiving in the first several years of life will ultimately grow into a mature brain that is less reactive and more capable of regulation and self-control.

As a result of the bottom-up pattern of brain development, and the impact of the emotional core on the development of the outer layers, the caregiving experiences of children link quite profoundly to numerous developmental outcomes. For example, children whose scripts about their caregivers suggest that the big person cannot always be counted on to respond to their needs are subsequently more susceptible to developing depression and anxiety than children whose scripts tell them that the big person can almost always be counted on. Children who feel secure will experience higher levels of positive mood and better coping strategies, as well as be more capable of regulating emotion.[11] In general, children who have had positive, secure, connected experiences of being cared for go on to be much more able to manage stress, much less vulnerable to mental health challenges, and generally much better "behaved" (eventually) due to their capacity to self-regulate.

Part of what allows children who experience consistent, nurturing, connection-informed caregiving to realize better outcomes is that this kind of caregiving allows them to feel safe in expressing their emotions—no matter how colorful, intense, or difficult. Children who feel "allowed" to express their emotions are necessarily children who truly believe that their big people will be capable of handling the expressed emotion, regardless of its form. And when big people receive this expressed emotion, even in the form of super-challenging behavior, calmly, capably, and with control and care, children do not have to work so hard to be "heard" and understood. As a result, these children, having been heard and understood, feel much "safer" emotionally, and in turn, will be more regulated and settled.

Imagine yourself as a child that feels heard, understood, safe, regulated, and settled. How likely are you to respond to disappointment or frustration with a long and lengthy meltdown? More likely, you are going to have a short burst of frustration followed by sad, soft tears because you have an absolute belief in your emotional safety with your big person. You know that your big person will accept your emotions and that you will be affirmed in feeling understood. Thus you will be able to release your frustration and see it convert quickly into soft sadness. That is, you will be in a relational space where you are able to be *vulnerable* by communicating your emotions and feelings. Oh, what a wonderful space for a child to live in! Soft sadness is a sign of acceptance, and acceptance in turn is a sign of openness to change, to shift, to move on. All of this is growth. So, of course, children growing up in this way are more adaptable in the face of challenging circumstances and have better developmental outcomes over time.

Imagine how a well-regulated child is going to look in adulthood! When you think about what you want most for the child or children you are growing up, whether you are a parent or another kind of big person, isn't that what you most hope for? That the child for whom you have some degree of responsibility in growing up will become an adult that is happy, settled, and contributing to the world? It is amazing to think that in the simple yet profound act of helping a child to grow a settled brain via consistent, nurturing care, you have such an extraordinary impact on the child's capacity to realize that kind of existence in adulthood.

It's important to note that sometimes in the process of imagining how your child is experiencing you as a caregiver and, more broadly, how he is experiencing the world, you can unwittingly feel echoes of your own childhood and hurts regarding your own unmet needs. This is a very common and normal response to have as a big person. In fact, many people who are activated about their own childhoods as they seek to be the best possible big person for their own children find their own past hurts finally addressed and soothed through a conscious awareness of such, and the ability and power to create a very different experience for their own children. In some cases, of course, the wounds are very deep. If this is the case for you, seek out helpful counseling support that enables you to resolve these past hurts so you can develop positive, caring relationships with your own children.

THE ART OF *BEING*

Not everyone who wants to help children has to become a child development psychology major or an expert about brain science. However, we now know so much about neuroplasticity and the connection between healthy brain development and optimal caregiving experiences that big people today really should have some awareness about it. When we know better, we do better.

Even a surface-level understanding of the interaction between brain development and caregiving can allow us to make better choices about discipline that are informed by facts. Then, in the loud and messy moments of yelly-shouty-hitting-meltdowns, and the slightly quieter ones too, we will be inspired by this knowledge to move quietly, confidently, and swiftly to create a day-to-day experience that is going to work well for our children's growing brains and their growing sense of self. The more often we respond to their needs and give them a positive calming experience, the more it accumulates at a neural level and writes for them a relationship script in which they know we can be counted on to understand them inherently. This is a script in which they are confident in our ability to meet their needs, a script in which they can feel understood, protected, and deeply and profoundly known. To create that kind of script, we have to have connection-informed responses to the challenging behaviors our children might display, and sculpt for them a world that works well for their growing little selves. That is the art of *being* for our children. And to be for our children, we first need to *feel* what it is like to walk a mile in their shoes. With that knowledge, we will find ourselves brilliantly positioned to respond to them in the ways that help regulate, grow brains, write healthy relationship scripts, and allow them to feel guided through the stresses of life. That is, in relying on our innate capacity as social beings, we will be able to meaningfully connect with our children and grow them up in the best possible way.

INSIDE THE DISCIPLINE VORTEX

We now know what happens in the brain when a child's stress is responded to calmly, with connection: the regulatory core of the brain is settled, the child feels secure in the knowledge that her needs will be met, and her challenging behaviors consequently become fewer and less intense. We also know that while it is possible to use disciplinary strategies such as time-outs, removal of privileges, and voiced disapproval to secure good behavior, their effect is based on fear, not connection, and the result is temporary. It is essentially a behavioral façade. And finally, we know that when a child experiences persistent disconnection from a special big person through these kinds of disciplinary practices, it results in continued stress and escalates connection-seeking behavioral responses (acting out), which are exacerbated when the child's big person again responds with disconnection-informed disciplinary strategies. We call this insidious cycle the discipline vortex.

THE DISCIPLINE VORTEX

What we need to remember is that the force of this vortex comes from the adult who drives the escalating behaviors in the child with discipline strategies that are based on disconnection. The child is just being and doing what children are developmentally meant to be and do. That is, it is not the child's behavior that needs to change. Rather, it is the adult's response to the child's attempt to communicate an unmet need that is the root of the problem. As we've seen, when the adult responds to the child's upset with connection, the entire cycle is halted. Connection allows for discipline without damage, and responsibility for connection is the big person's to own. To understand exactly how the discipline vortex works, to know exactly when you have entered it, and, if you have, how to get out of it, consider the case of Sophia and the troublesome trampoline.

CASE STUDY: SOPHIA & THE TROUBLESOME TRAMPOLINE

Seven-year-old Sophia was on her way home from a long day of school, and all she really wanted to do was get on her trampoline and jump. As her mom was pulling the family car into the garage to park, Sophia was already envisioning her next steps. She'd grab her backpack, race inside, drop her lunch bag onto the kitchen counter, and head out the back door. If she was really lucky, she'd be jumping on the trampoline in less than sixty seconds.

Also in the car that day were Sophia's older brother, Sam, who was in Grade 5, and a friend of his. The boys had had a long day at school too, and unbeknownst to Sophia, they also had designs on the trampoline. They had conspired over recess and were keen to take up where they had left off with their last game of crack-the-egg. Sam liked it most when he got to be "the egg," all curled up in a ball on the trampoline, as his friend tried to bounce around enough that he'd "crack the egg" and Sam's arms and legs would fly open.

As the car came to a stop and everybody jumped out, the calamity began. Sam and his friend made it inside first. Sophia stopped to say hello to the cat and arrived in the kitchen just in time to see Sam and his friend fly out the back door, obviously en route to the trampoline. Sophia's heart fell. She knew the rule. When her brother had a friend over, she had to give them space to hang out. And she also knew that only 2 people were allowed on the trampoline at a time. Just like that—*poof!*—there went her afterschool trampoline dream... unless she was able to convince Sam that she really should have got the first turn.

Sophia headed out the back door shouting to Sam, "I wanted to go on the trampoline. No fair!!! I thought of it first!" Sam, emboldened a little by the presence of his friend, hollered back, "You snooze you lose, Sophia! We were here first. You have to wait your turn!" Sophia was mad. "That's not fair, Sam," she yelled. "You ALWAYS take first turn, and today it's my turn to go first!!!" Sam told Sophia to be quiet and go away. But Sophia wasn't going to let Sam be the boss of her, and without a moment's hesitation she swooped down, scooped up a pair of Sam's runners that were by the back door, and deftly lobbed them one by one onto the trampoline, bouncing one off Sam's shoulder and landing the second one on Sam's leg. Just at that moment, Sam and Sophia's mom wandered into the kitchen, in time to hear Sam screeching at Sophia.

FREEZE! Sophia's mother now has the job of figuring out the situation. What would you do? To explain the inner workings of discipline, let's consider a few different options for Sophia's mother. The first ones reflect the dominant parenting pop culture, while the final option reveals connection as the answer.

☛ Option 1: time-out

Sophia's mother is fed up with this kind of behavior from Sophia. Ms. Smith forcefully opens the back door and commands, "Sophia! Come. Here. Now." Sophia shuffles over, trying to keep some distance between herself and her mother, and squeezes inside the house. "What were you thinking?" her mother is saying. "Sam has a friend over and you could have hurt that boy, never mind how dangerous that is for your brother! How many times do I have to tell you to keep your temper under control?! You are almost 8 years old, Sophia, and this is simply unacceptable. You will spend the rest of Sam's playdate in your room. You are only allowed to come out to use the bathroom. Do you understand?" At this point, Sophia starts to cry, and her mother continues, "Do not start with that, Sophia. Your tears will not change a single thing. Off to your room with you. Now." Sophia, still crying, heads off to her room and closes the door. Ms. Smith, thankful for the reprieve, starts unpacking the lunches, making dinner, and calling the vet to make an appointment for the cat.

☛ Option 2: reward chart

Sophia's mother has noticed that her daughter seems to be a lot more fiery than many of her friends of the same age, and Ms. Smith is worried that Sophia's reactive behaviors when frustrated mean she may be lagging behind her peers in emotional growth and development. Her mother is not certain that she has done enough to help Sophia, and she has some concerns around disciplinary measures such as time-outs that seem to emphasize punishment rather than praise. Ms. Smith pokes her head out the back door and quietly asks Sophia to come into the kitchen. She sits Sophia down and firmly reminds her daughter that this kind of behavior must stop. She then pulls out some paper and stickers as she says, "I think you might need some help to remember that you cannot behave this way, so we are going to create a star chart for you that we will hang on the fridge. You can decorate it any way you want. For every day that you do not shout, throw, or try to hurt your brother, you will get to put a star on the chart right before bedtime. If, at the end of the week you have collected 5 or more stars, I will give you $5 that you can spend however you choose." After her mother draws the grid, fills in the days of the week, and labels it "Sophia's Good Behavior Chart," she leaves Sophia at the counter to decorate it while she puts away the groceries.

☛ Option 3: consequences

Sophia's mother believes that her daughter is stubborn beyond comprehension and utterly unable to accept no for an answer or to be flexible in any kind of problem solving. As a parent, she feels she must drive home the point once and for all that this kind of behavior is absolutely unworkable and will not be tolerated. Ms. Smith knows just how much Sophia loves looming: her daughter has created all sorts of lovely charms and bracelets for everybody in the family—and even in the neighborhood. Ms. Smith squares her shoulders, opens the back door, and says to Sophia, "You have got to stop with this. It cannot happen even one more time. You are almost 8 years old. Five-year-olds act this way but not 8-year-olds. It is time you learned a lesson. I have decided to take away your Rainbow Loom® for a full week." Sophia's face crumples into tears as she sobs, "That's not fair, Mom! Sam started this. Sam should have a consequence too!!!!" "Sam did not throw shoes at you," her mother replies quietly. "And I am the mother here. You are not. Go and get me all of your looming stuff. I will not hear another word. Off with you." Sophia marches off to her room to retrieve her beloved looming supplies in order to hand them over to her mother.

☛ Option 4: grounding

Sophia's mother is embarrassed that the other neighborhood parents can hear her almost-8-year-old child behaving this way. With a forced breath and a roll of her eyes, Ms. Smith flies out the back door and demands that Sophia get in the house. Sophia can tell her mom is really mad and scampers past her. Her mother turns on her heel, marches back into the house, and barks, "Sophia, enough! We had almost the exact same problem yesterday. And the day before that you threw your brother's backpack at him. It is like every day there is another thing. And I will not tolerate it for another second. You are grounded. And by that I mean no friends, no park, no dance class, no nothing for 5 days. I should make it 8 days since you ARE almost 8 years old, for goodness sake! But 5 days it is, and I won't hear a single word of whining about it. Have I made myself clear?!" Sophia nods, seemingly resigned to her fate. Her mother feels a small sense of triumph but wonders what she is going to do with Sophia for the next 5 days. Such are the costs of good parenting, she believes.

☛ Option 5: removal of privilege

Sophia's mother cannot understand why her daughter cannot just learn to take a deep breath, calmly state her case, and ask for help if she needs it. Sophia, she feels, needs to act her age and learn responsibility for herself and her behavior. Ms. Smith tells Sophia to come into the kitchen immediately, and explains, "Sophia, this is ridiculous and it has got to stop. What are you going to do when you are twenty-seven and someone you work with gets to the photocopier first?! Are you going to throw something at them? You have got to learn this lesson once and for all. You cannot throw stuff. It is dangerous. It hurts people. And most of all, it is not what almost-8-year-olds do; it is what 3-year-olds do. I have decided that every time you act like a 3-year-old, I will treat you like one. And 3-year-olds don't get to choose a family meal—obviously they are too immature to do that. So for this week you will not choose what the family eats for dinner on Tuesday as you usually do. Keep up this behavior and I will cancel Thursday as well." Sophia is utterly crestfallen: one of her most favorite things is her special family meal days. No more mac 'n' cheese night for her this week. "Fine, what*ever*," she sulks, and heads off to be by herself in her room.

☛ Option 6: connection

Sophia's mother understands that her daughter is disappointed at not being able to do what she had her heart set on. Ms. Smith zooms outside as fast as she can, looks quickly to see that Sophia's hands are free of projectiles, and then places a gentle hand on Sophia's arm as she calls out to Sam and his friend to make sure they're okay. Once she's sure they're all right, Ms. Smith says to Sophia, "My sweet girl, it looks to me like you are having a tough go. Come inside with me, let me grab you a drink of water, and let's figure this out. I am sure we can find a way to have it feel better." With a caring arm around her daughter's shoulders, Sophia's mom adeptly guides them back into the house as she empathizes, "It's hard to be the younger sister sometimes, isn't it? You had your heart set on jumping on the trampoline, didn't you sweetie, and you just need some help to figure out what to do about all of that, right?" As they snuggle close, Sophia's mom rubs her daughter's back and says gently, "I've got you now. You're okay. We're okay," and Sophia's hot, frustrated tears become softer and eventually subside. As Sophia slurps some water, Ms. Smith reassures Sophia that she can have some trampoline time once the boys finish their turn. She sets the timer on the kitchen stove for fifteen minutes so Sophia is certain that her time to jump will finally come.

Feeling much more hopeful and also much calmer, Sophia decides to do some looming on her beloved Rainbow Loom® to pass the time. As she settles into this activity, Ms. Smith comments on what a remarkable eye Sophia has for picking out just the right color combinations for the different creations she makes. And as Sophia smiles at the compliment, her mom adds, "Honey, we probably need to talk really quickly about what happened with your brother. I know you were disappointed and I know it is hard. But it is so important that we find ways to solve problems with your brother that don't involve hurting his heart or hurting his body. Can I count on you to remember that next time around?" Sophia nods sincerely, and her mom continues. "When you are ready—maybe after Sam's friend leaves to go home—perhaps you can find a quick second to say sorry for the shoe throwing too." She plants a caring kiss on Sophia's forehead and carries on with unloading the car from the day's activities.

SOPHIA'S CASE DISSECTED

Sophia responded to the disappointment of not being able to jump on the trampoline like a lot of almost-8-year-old children might after a long day at school. She was likely tired and low on coping reserves. That she blew up at her brother is not surprising or troubling. Sophia was just communicating a need: she was disappointed, overwhelmed by frustration, and could not sort out a workable solution in that state. In short, Sophia was very disregulated. And all of that makes perfect sense when considered developmentally and through Sophia's eyes. In fact, Sophia's real troubles from a developmental perspective didn't actually begin until the point at which her mother chose how to respond to Sophia's behavior in the various scenarios. Let's take a look at what was really happening in each of the responses.

☞ The problem with option 1: time-out

In this first response, Sophia's mother is exasperated with Sophia because she does not understand that the real purpose of Sophia's behavior is an unmet need. First, Sophia's mother begins the interaction with Sophia in a loud, stern voice, which likely further disregulates her already disappointed, frustrated daughter. Second, by using phrases such as "What were you thinking?" or "You are almost 8 years old!," Ms. Smith is effectively shaming Sophia. And following with phrases like "How many times do I have to tell you?" just highlights for Sophia that the special big person she is counting on is unable to shift Sophia's behavior, which may lead Sophia to believe that her mother is not really in charge. In other words, Ms. Smith cannot be depended on to meet Sophia's needs. So, so far, Sophia has had no reassurance that her need will be met or that she is safe and secure and connected to her mother. To compound the disconnection, Sophia is sent off to her bedroom, further separating her from that much-needed connection with her mother. And as Sophia begins to cry—effectively revealing emotion—her mother rebuffs that vulnerability with stinging comments such as "Your tears will not change a single thing." What this says to Sophia is that her mother cannot understand or manage these messy emotions and therefore it is not safe for her to express them. What began as a simple unmet need—disappointment at not being able to jump on the trampoline—has now, through disconnected disciplinary actions, mushroomed into a series of damaging social-emotional messages that could potentially lead to harmful outcomes over time. This is the discipline vortex at work.

☞ The problem with option 2: reward chart

Sophia's mother approaches this situation with the best of intentions. She is clearly concerned about Sophia's explosiveness when frustrated, and in describing her daughter as more "fiery," it sounds as if Ms. Smith is attuned to the fact that Sophia may be more "sensitive" than other children her age. However, she does not acknowledge to Sophia that she understands the real reason for her behavior—the unmet need of wanting to jump on the trampoline. And she does not hold her daughter or reassure her that it's okay to feel frustrated; instead, she focuses on correcting the behavior. From Sophia's perspective, her mother is disconnected—she's not shaming or berating or using time-outs, but she is still withholding physical and emotional closeness and making the eventual provision of these—via praise and the reward chart—contingent on something else (good behavior) rather than unconditional. Ms. Smith mentions that she is not certain "she has done enough" for Sophia, and her daughter is likely experiencing not only the disconnection but her mother's doubt about her parenting ability. In other words, Sophia has no assurance that her mother can and will meet her needs, and further, has some worry now of being able to live up to the demands of the reward chart in order to secure praise.

The glossy façade of a reward chart lures Ms. Smith in, and she is duped into believing that associating a reward with an action will support her child in internalizing that action. First, however, as we know, the withholding of reward is a disconnecting kind of action: this is the seedy underbelly of a reward chart's glossy façade. Second, no external thing like a reward can ever build the neural pathways necessary for self-regulation and true independence. And finally, we do not want our children to behave well because they get something for it; we want the desire to interact kindly with the world around them to bubble up from somewhere deep inside. Until Ms. Smith nurtures her daughter with connection and helps Sophia cultivate the neurological growth that results in the capacity for self-control, Ms. Smith will continue to be drawn into the discipline vortex.

☞ *The problem with option 3: consequences*

In this scenario, Ms. Smith seems to be at her wit's end. She describes her daughter as "stubborn beyond comprehension" and inflexible in any kind of problem solving, which suggests that she sees these traits as faults rather than as natural stages of development. Sophia's brain is not quite developed enough to regulate her responses, but this is entirely normal for her age and temperament. As with options 1 and 2, Sophia's mom has not acknowledged that she understands the real reason for her daughter's upset. That sets up the initial disconnect. Ms. Smith then shames her daughter by comparing her to a 5-year-old. And finally, in using her knowledge of Sophia's favorite and cherished activity against Sophia, Ms. Smith is also inadvertently engaging in and exacerbating the disconnect.

Ms. Smith's focus on hammering home the point to Sophia that her behavior needs to change is born of a misguided understanding of behavior. Acting out is a child's attempt to communicate an unmet need, and to change the behavior the need must be met. It cannot simply be stamped out by a forceful consequence. In contrast, meeting a child's needs consistently champions the development of self-regulation and leads to less challenging behavior down the road. Sometimes it can help to adjust the conditions in a child's day-to-day world—for example, setting a schedule for trampoline-jumping or spending extra time with Mom or Dad—to further accommodate a more regulated state. Similar to the previous 2 scenarios, here Sophia's need for connection, reassurance, and understanding have not been met, which just perpetuates the discipline vortex.

☛ The problem with option 4: grounding

Ms. Smith is struggling with her own regulation in this scenario. She is upset by the idea that others in her neighborhood might be disapproving of her child's behavior and, in turn, of her as a mother. The "forced breath," the "roll of her eyes," and the demand for Sophia's attention all reveal that Ms. Smith is not actually a take-charge, capable kind of big person. Sophia senses this and is not feeling connected to or regulated by her mother. On the contrary, she is trying to escape any physical contact with Ms. Smith by "scampering" past her. Sophia seems scared rather than settled. In lamenting that "everyday there is just another thing," Ms. Smith paints Sophia as beyond hope, and this utterly disconnecting and deflating attitude is likely communicated to Sophia subtly and/or overtly in her mother's other day-to-day actions. Since Sophia is already experiencing such a high level of emotional and physical disconnect from her mother, alongside a niggling knowledge that Ms. Smith cannot and will not meet Sophia's needs, the actual disciplinary action just deepens and entrenches that certainty. Ms. Smith is once more playing her connection with Sophia and her knowledge of Sophia's likes against her daughter. The result—Sophia's quiet resignation to her fate—is heart-breaking. Her spirit has been broken and her emotions deadened, as her disregulated brain scrambles to deal with the cacophony of upset it is experiencing.

☛ The problem with option 5: removal of privilege

As with option 4, Ms. Smith is frustrated! In this scenario, Ms. Smith's disregulation overshadows her ability to see her daughter's unmet need and social-emotional reality. To start, she is grossly overestimating the ability of Sophia's brain. As we've seen, Sophia's reaction to the trampoline incident, especially if she is indeed sensitive, is entirely normal for her age and temperament. Throwing shoes at her brother and his friend further confirms that what Sophia needs is regulation and connection. However, instead of reassuring her daughter, Ms. Smith shames Sophia by demoting her to the status of a 3-year-old and withholding her usual privileges as an 8-year-old. From Sophia's perspective, these actions just deepen the social and emotional disconnect between her mother and herself. In fact, her "Fine, what*ever*" response is a defensive reaction to prevent the hurt from her mother's actions from becoming too much. The fact that Sophia goes to her bedroom shows us that Ms. Smith's reaction had Sophia moving in exactly the *wrong* direction. Instead of seeking connection in her moment of need, Sophia has been given the message that no connection is available and so she hides away—maybe hugging a much-loved stuffy or playing with a much-loved toy—instead of getting the connection she really *needs:* connection with her mom. Again, this is another example of that insidious cycle, the discipline vortex, in action.

☞ *The secret of success in option 6: connection!*

In this scenario, Sophia's mother understands Sophia as a child who has needs, a child who is struggling. Everything about Ms. Smith's response to her daughter appears solidly grounded in a truly instinctive under-standing of child development. Ms. Smith takes control of the situation swiftly, making sure that everyone is safe and okay while simultaneously connecting with Sophia in her body language, tone of voice, and choice of words. She calms Sophia's activated system by communicating that she understands Sophia, by validating Sophia's feelings, and by physi-cally comforting Sophia. In getting Sophia a drink of water, Ms. Smith is both taking care of Sophia and also distracting her physical senses, which can help children to regulate a bit more and prevent them from getting stuck on a single thought, in this case Sophia's frustration with her brother.

What's happening from Sophia's perspective? As she connects with her mom, Sophia is able to feel some sadness about what happened, which is a whole lot better than frustration. By feeling sad, Sophia can begin to let go of her anger and disappointment, which allows her mind to regulate more effectively and become more open to considering alter-native outcomes. Instead of focusing on the trampoline, she gravitates to looming. And in a moment of calm connection when her mother "joins" with Sophia in looming and offers her daughter a compliment, the two are able to cement their connection. They are now very much on the same page, and Ms. Smith can then very quickly deliver some instruction about how Sophia can handle the situation better next time around and communicate her belief in Sophia's ability to deliver on this. Instead of hearing this information as shaming, Sophia is regulated. She has a plan for next time. And she believes deeply in her mother's understanding of her needs and in her mother's ability to absolutely "have her back." When her mom kisses Sophia's forehead, the emotional connection is further sealed and an end is subtly signaled, sort of like saying, "Constructive feedback time is over and connection is the name of the game."

It's important to remember that challenging behavior is normal for children. The reason that option 6 is effective is because, in this scenario, Sophia's mother recognizes that regular child development includes impulsive, unregulated, and intense behavior, and forces no disconnection upon her. On the contrary, Ms. Smith acknowledges the challenging behavior and all the messy emotions and needs around it, embraces it, and allows it to diffuse naturally. That's why connection works—because it breaks the discipline vortex.

THE ORIGINS OF BEHAVIOR

Children's behavior is often classified as "good" or "bad" without taking into account its origin. Where the impulses for those actions arise is important in helping us to understand how to address them. If you were to take up residence in a neighborhood park, a classroom, or any other environment where you could observe children of various ages, try to log all of their "misbehavior," and then figure out the cause of those behaviors, you would quickly realize they derive from 2 sources: 1) normal child development and 2) the disconnect. To understand behavior as the result of these two sources, we will look at normal development at different ages, and then at the effect of the disciplinary disconnect on subsequent behaviors.

☛ Normal child development

The way children act is a result of both the degree to which their brains have developed and the process of individuation. Therefore, to understand what is "normal behavior" and what is not, it is necessary to look at the influence of each of these factors.

INFANTS (UP TO 2 YEARS OLD). In newborn babies, the neural pathways responsible for social-emotional communication, regulation, and impulse control are all very immature. For this reason, infants are not typically thought of by big people as wilfully engaging in misbehavior. Indeed, their brains require a significant amount of external regulation by big people. As babies are nurtured and tended to in very caring and responsive ways, their brains begin the long process of developing the capacity to regulate independently. Research suggests that there is created "a set of specific sensory stimuli which are translated into specific neural activations in areas of the developing brain destined to become responsible for socio-emotional communication and bonding."[1] That is, nurturing care gets encoded into the neurons of an infant's brain and allows that infant the opportunity to grow into a child, and eventually an adult, who can regulate and happily coexist with other human beings. While this important neuroinfrastructure is being sculpted, the baby has only just begun the process of individuation. This early in life, and up until around a child's second birthday, the child thinks of herself as the same being as her big person, so tightly does the baby's sense of self depend on the big person. There is not a lot of need for such a little being to assert her independence.

Even though infants require significant co-regulation and are incredibly dependent on their big people for their sense of self, it is still widely believed that infants wilfully manipulate their circumstances to control different situations. For example, the Ferber method of sleep training recommends that parents "extinguish" their instinct to respond to their infants' cries so the babies can "learn" to fall asleep on their own or "self-soothe" to sleep. As one popular parenting website described: "After a few days to a week of gradually increasing the waiting time, the theory goes, most babies learn to fall asleep on their own, having discovered that crying earns nothing more than a brief check from you." Words like "earn" suggest that infants are actually making those connections, and by extension that they previously held an "ill-advised" understanding that crying would make you come. It is language like this, which still lurks in parenting pop culture, that suggests babies are purposefully concocting unreasonable pitches to make us hold them longer.

What *is* normal for infants is that they cry out and become fussy whenever they have a need—big or small! Cries are the only means of communication they have to signal their need for you. And your prompt attention to this expressed need, and your ongoing nurturing touch and presence, is exactly what their brains require to grow for them that most essential foundation.

TODDLERS (2 TO 3 YEARS OLD). In toddlers, the brain's prefrontal and frontal cortex is still relatively immature, and full development of those layers is several years off. This means that a toddler's impulse control, and most versions of what we identify as self-control, are not yet possible. As far as the process of individuation goes, toddlers continue to think of themselves largely in the terms created for them by their big people.

Typical toddler behaviors reflect an emerging and newfound sense of independence. They often discover the word "no" and use it to oppose many of the requests you might make of them. Although the intensity and frequency of behavior is affected by a child's individual temperament, it is entirely normal at this stage to experience lots of meltdowns, screaming, tears, and tantrums because the capacity for self-regulation is only just emerging. Toddlers often have the best of intentions to do as you ask but they cannot yet hold on to more than one significant idea at a time, a capacity that developmental psychologist and author Dr. Gordon Neufeld refers to as "mix."[2] This capacity only begins to emerge around ages 5 to 7 for most children, and even later for children who are intense or sensitive. Due to this lack of self-control, toddlers can be physically aggressive, lash out, and act impulsively. What they need from big people at this time is lots of nurturing care to help develop their neural pathways and their capacity for self-regulation.

PRESCHOOLERS (3 TO 4 YEARS OLD). Preschoolers are typically more able than toddlers to regulate around frustration and upset, although they continue to require a lot of external regulation from their special big people. Preschoolers also have a more established sense of self, which leads them to be more curious around testing limits and exploring, as well as wanting more room for personal wants and preferences. Preschoolers are still impulsive and find self-control elusive in more challenging moments, such as having to share. They can be aggressive, although the combination of a higher ability to regulate and an increased capacity to use language and words to communicate typically reduces the frequency and the intensity of these aggressive behaviors. Once again, children who are generally more intense and/or sensitive will need longer for their brains to be able to regulate to a degree that matches their intensity/sensitivity. Preschoolers still need a lot of help from their special big people to grow their brains, pattern the networks for self-regulation, and meet their needs for connection.

5- TO 7-YEAR-OLDS. By the time they start school, children are continuing to develop their self-identity and independence. They start to see themselves not as just the person their parent has created but as a creation of both themselves and their parent. They express their own preferences vociferously and increasingly explore their own interests. And they are better able to regulate their own behavior except when they are upset, tired, or overwhelmed. At these times, you should still expect some meltdowns and outbursts that will need the gentle care of a special big person to settle and calm the situation.

The frontal and prefrontal cortex are typically developed enough to allow some tentative attempts at "self-control." In other words, 5- to 7-year-olds are starting to be able to hold 2 ideas in mind at the same time and choose the "right" idea over the other one. For example, as we sat in the plane waiting to take off for home after a wild, crazy, fun, and exhausting week of family vacation in Disneyland, one of my sons, who was 6, said, "Mommy, I am so glad to be going home but I am so sad to be leaving Disneyland." As only a psychologist would do, I did my internal happy dance to see this lovely expression of the first signs of "mixing." He really wanted to get back to the comfort of home and, at the same time, he didn't want to leave behind the rides and the treats and the animated characters that had captured his imagination at Disneyland. He experienced both the idea of being excited to go home and the idea of being sad to leave California at the same time, and he was able to acknowledge the 2 seemingly contrary ideas hanging out together in his frontal cortex—the mix!

Once children can consider 2 very different options or ideas simultaneously, they have the underpinnings of self-control because they have at least a hope of choosing the more "appropriate" one. In the schoolyard, this is usually the start of seeing kids begin to share successfully. They understand that they may want a toy but that getting it would require pushing over another child and making that child cry, and so they ultimately exercise control in not pushing over the other child. At this stage, however, intense feelings will still overwhelm this ability, making one idea more prominent, pushing the other into submission, and—*poof!*—hello impulse and goodbye self-control!

8- TO 10-YEAR-OLDS. By the time they are 8, children are more independent than ever in wanting to explore all that is new and interesting and express themselves for who they are and what makes them unique. They have their own sense of style and want to pick out their own clothes. They gravitate to certain musical artists or bands. They pursue a passion for a particular sport or art or science. They like making their own decisions about their meals and snacks. Sometimes they may go too far, overstepping boundaries and needing some supervision or guidance around that. Children in this age range are also very much more able to regulate, although when taxed or overwhelmed they may occasionally have outbursts, meltdowns, or bouts of tears. That's when they still need the support and care of a special big person to help them manage these big emotions. And while they want and desire freedom to be who it is that they are becoming, children in this age range still need at-a-distance supervision for routine activities. Aggressive acting out should be largely subsiding for this age group except in times of intensity and usually just with people they know well (e.g., siblings). As well, this age is typically all about "me," and thus, this is a stage at which children are often so wrapped up in their own interests and ideas that they can sometimes seem to lack empathy and compassion for others.

11- TO 12-YEAR-OLDS.[3] Preteens are even more independent than 8- to 10-year-olds, and they are more forceful in wanting to state their opinions, take a stand, and push the boundaries. Their idealized outlook on the world and life can sometimes lead them into risky or unsafe situations, and so you will often find yourself setting, holding, and negotiating rules. Children in this age range love to "discuss" things, and are becoming increasingly intent on stating their opinions and backing them up with well-reasoned facts and ideas. Children at this age can seem deliberately rebellious as they choose clothing styles, hair colors, and other forms of self-expression that seem specifically selected to cause upset, but are really just about individuation.

Hormonal fluctuations and changes in brain chemistry and organization can lead to some extreme moods and behaviors at times. Peers are also becoming more prominent influences. However, in this time of flux, your children still very much need you and will benefit from time spent with you, and more generally, your physical and emotional presence.

13- TO 17-YEAR-OLDS. By the time most children are teenagers, the frontal and prefrontal cortex of their brain will have reached full thickness. Some fine-tuning is still needed around impulse control, especially because of brain and hormonal changes that are often occurring concurrently. Typically, this leads to the "moodiness" usually associated with teenagers, but you will not encounter the meltdowns and tantrums of the past, and only the occasional aggressive outburst or argument. At this age, young people continue to be strongly independent, idealistic, and black-and-white thinkers. They still want to take risks, assert their opinions, and push boundaries. All of this behavior is very normal. In spite of their increasingly adult-like appearance and actions, children in this age group are still children and they do still need the safe and nurturing presence of big people in their lives, guiding the way and calming rough waters as needed.

Children behave as they do because they are following the normal patterns of brain development. It is not because they are trying to make you crazy, push your buttons, or manipulate situations. Instead it is because *that is how they are supposed to behave given the development of their brains and their sense of self.* When a child engages in a behavior, it isn't a personal affront or a direct hit aimed at your heart. Instead, it is just a child being and doing and growing up in the way that nature intended.

☞ The disconnect

If you watch children interact in their neighborhood parks or class-rooms over a prolonged period, you start to see how the second source of behavior is "the disconnect." It comes about because of big-person actions or life situations that create emotional or physical divides between children and their big people. This is a dynamic I have seen play out in my own home many times.

I have a very distinct memory of my son Nathan watching me pre-pare to leave for a work trip when he was about 5 years old. As I gathered my suitcase and other belongings at the door, I felt a dull thud as one of his action figures hit me in the back of the head and fell to the floor. I turned around to see what was happening, just as a second action figure came flying through the air. I quickly realized that he was launching them one by one, intent on unloading the whole basket. What had set this off, I wondered? It seemed to have come out of nowhere. But, of course, it had not come out of nowhere. It had come from somewhere very profound and important. In facing a physical disconnect from me, Nathan was upset: his stress response center was fired up and releasing "fight-or-flight" hormones into his body. As much as Nathan might try to regulate his behavior, his body was being overwhelmed and escalating its connection-seeking response so that his special big person—me—could meet his need for external support in the face of this emotional intensity.

To create a sense of containment and safety for him, I stated gently but firmly, "That needs to stop," as another action figure was hurled my way. And then I moved swiftly towards him, acknowledging in a passionate, empathetic tone that it was obvious to me that he was struggling. I mused aloud how hard it must be for him to know that I was leaving, and that he was not coming with me. I suggested that my going might be even harder than usual since I was on my way to a place where we had previously vaca-tioned together as a family. By now I had him next to me, and I was down on the floor beside him, talking calmly and compassionately. "You really miss me when I am gone, don't you?" I affirmed. "You really want to come and it is hard knowing that you can't, isn't it?" And slowly but surely Nathan's anger melted into tears, and he folded his sweet self into my lap and cried. I held him and calmed him and came up with a plan for having him feel like he could hold on to me even though I would not be there physically. And ultimately he was able to manage my departure in a safe, if sad, mindset.

What this example shows is that children cannot help but be activated in the face of a disconnect. The response is hardwired into their brains and bodies; remember, the ultimate fear of all children everywhere is that they might lose us, their big people. Our children's activated response in the face of a disconnect is not reasoned, it is purely *mechanistic*—that is, the brain and the psyche just go there. It is so instinctual, in fact, that this response actually happens before our children even realize it. And it results equally, whether the disconnect is physical (as in the case of Nathan having to say goodbye to me) or emotional (as in the following examples). Just stand near the checkout counter at a grocery store, and you'll see. Watch what happens when a parent in the lineup with a child or two in tow turns on his phone and tries to send a text message. It won't be long before the children begin to squabble or rearrange the checkout displays or peek into the baskets of surrounding customers, as the full force of the emotional disconnect settles in. Or see what happens when a parent helping her child complete some math homework starts to struggle with her own frustration around having to do Grade 5 math again. As soon as the child catches even the slightest whiff of a parental sigh or a tensed jaw, the child's behavior will shift as a direct, subconscious, mechanistic reaction to the disconnect.

WHAT'S A BIG PERSON TO DO?

In dominant parenting pop culture, our belief is that when a child exhibits "bad" behavior of any kind, we big people are supposed to do something

about it. After all, goes the prevailing logic, children need to learn the lessons that will prepare them to be successful in adulthood. It is this thinking
that sucks us into the discipline vortex. In a nutshell, the child acts a certain
way, then the adult responds with a "traditional" or "popularized" response
to the behavior—just like Sophia and her mother in the scenarios we looked
at earlier in the chapter. The problem is that all of these responses create
an experience of disconnection for the child. And the continued activation
that accompanies this disconnection often leads to acting out, which, in
turn, is likely to be responded to with traditional forms of discipline in
order to be "fixed." Thus the vortex grabs hold: disconnection answered
with disconnection leads to activation in the child. If responded to with yet
more disconnection, the whole thing takes on a life of its own. In order to
steer clear of the discipline vortex, it sometimes helps to better understand
the manner in which big people are often first sucked in.

HOW WE ENTER THE DISCIPLINE VORTEX

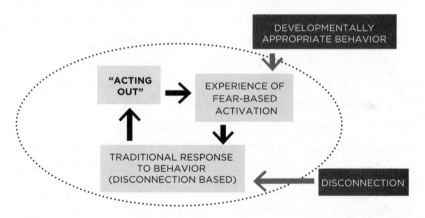

☛ *Entering the discipline vortex*

The idea of imposing disconnection in discipline likely goes back, at
least in part, to the historical views in which evil must be purged from

children at all costs, and good must be injected at all costs. Additionally, when we think of children as miniature versions of adults, we may be tempted to discipline them using methods derived from adult behaviors such as shunning or ostracism that intentionally create an emotional and/or physical divide to coax individuals and/or groups into compliance and/or prevent divergence. Not only do these methods not create lasting behavioral changes in children (nor in adults for that matter), they are also potentially damaging both to the child's developing brain and to the child's developing sense of self.

As we begin to get sucked deeper and deeper into the discipline vortex, our children's behaviors continue because big people are causing them to exist through their traditional pop culture approaches to discipline. To discipline without damage, big people must escape the vortex. And to escape the vortex, big people must stop using the disconnect as a disciplinary technique. By taking this step, we have ultimate control—we can re-establish connection and stop the cycle.

HOW WE ESCAPE THE DISCIPLINE VORTEX

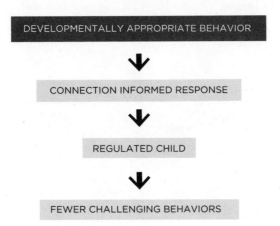

☛ Escaping the discipline vortex

Pulling out of the vortex and going back to the child's innate need for connection allows us to find how children need us to *be* in the face of "misbehavior." We've seen that they need their big people all the way through their developmental journey. We've confirmed that they will naturally yell, push, hit, tantrum, and behave in challenging ways from the time they are infants right up until they become adults, and that these behaviors are normal and expected. So it is up to us to shift our thinking. Rather than punishing these behaviors and seeking to extinguish them at all costs, we need to think of them as essential to development. And in giving these varied behaviors the freedom and the room to exist, we must also recognize our children's extraordinary need for us to support them through any and all behavior. Our job is to meet their need: to regulate them, to bolster their emerging sense of self, and to script for them the idea of a world in which they are safe to express themselves freely because we "have their backs." Our responsibility is to climb out of the discipline vortex and back into the nurturing folds of connection. Our obligation to our children is to *see* the value in connection, *feel* it confidently and powerfully, and *be* it for our infants, toddlers, preschoolers, 5- to 7-year-olds, preteens, and teenagers, as only a big person can.

HULKING IT UP

When something is not working out for us, what all human beings really desire is someone who can be in charge, someone who can step in and confidently navigate whatever it is that feels so overwhelming or undoing. For children this is not only a desire, it is an essential *need*. Children are dependent upon big people by nature, and so, when they sense that the people who are meant to be in charge really are not all that in charge, children get worried. The more worried they get, the more they are driven to feel the security of having someone in charge. And most often, if nobody steps into the lead when they so desperately *need* someone to, they end up electing themselves to the position. The task of growing up children who are in the lead position is incredibly challenging. To better understand this dynamic, consider what happens when we as big people lose confidence in the experts who are meant to be guiding us.

CAPABILITY & CONFIDENCE

Do you remember the last time you were disappointed by someone you were really depending on to provide you with "expert" care, service, or advice? For example, imagine that you are really sick and miserable, that you have had a long, difficult night, and that you arrive at a walk-in medical clinic. You are intent on getting in to see the doctor as quickly as possible so you can get back to the comfort of home. At the reception counter, you give the attending clerk your name, which she adds to a list, and then you sit down in the waiting room. You look around and take stock of just how many people are waiting. In this first-come, first-served clinic, you make a mental note of who's ahead of you. And as the clock ticks, you watch others come in, put their names on the list, and sit down. Every few minutes you go over your own mental list of who is ahead of you and who is behind.

You have been waiting about forty-five minutes by the time the last of the people "in front of you" on the list gets called in to see the doctor. You are next! Finally! Your nausea, fever, and crazy fatigue are wearing you down, and you can't wait to see the doctor, come up with a diagnosis and treatment plan, and go back to bed. As the clerk grabs a file and stands up to call the next patient in, you reach down to grab your bag, readying yourself. But the name she calls is *not yours*. Immediately your mind is reeling. How could this be? Doesn't the clerk know that the man she just called came in *after* you? How could she have messed this up? So you march up to the counter and tell the clerk in no uncertain terms that you thought you were next. Can she confirm where you are on the list?

As the clerk shuffles through the files, you hear her mutter "whoops" under her breath. She turns to you and apologizes, but without a lot of care or feeling. She says that she misfiled you in the lineup, is sorry for the trouble, and dismissively invites you to take a seat until she can call you next. You, feeling less than endeared to the clerk at this point, ignore her invitation to sit and instead hover right next to the desk to make sure she doesn't forget her promise. True to her word, she calls you next. You head in to see the doctor, and the situation ends. Or does it?

☛ The mental shift

The medical clerk's mistake has shaken your confidence in her ability to do her job. You suspect she is not really all that "expert," though it's not a thought that you are actively processing as you talk with the doctor, as you head home afterwards, or even that you are likely to think or talk about again as the rest of the week unfolds. But rest assured, this shift in your mindset has occurred mechanistically—without effort or conscious awareness—and the next time you find yourself back in that waiting room, you are going to be very vigilant about the order in which patients are called in to see the doctor. Next time, right from the start, you are going to sit very close to the clerk's desk. And as you see the number of people before you on the list dwindle to the last person, you are going to stand up and head on over to talk with the clerk, casually but firmly stating to her that you "just want to make sure" that you are indeed next on the list.

Why will you take this tack next time? Why will you not be content to just sit and let the situation play out, allowing the clerk to do her job? You will do so because of "the shift." When your mind mechanistically demoted the clerk to a position of non-expert, it also denied her the assumptions that it makes about "experts": that she knew how to do her job and would do it well. In effect, as she became ineffective and incapable in your mind, you committed to being one step ahead of her, as you had lost faith in her ability to do right by you.

This exact same dynamic plays out with our children. In fact, this dynamic plays out in all relationships, adult or child. But the unique character of the big person–child relationship is that there are set roles regarding who is in charge and who is dependent. In most healthy adult relationships, there is some back and forth: for example, at times you are the nurturer whereas at other times your friend or spouse is the nurturer. In the big person–child relationship, there is not, cannot be, and should not ever be any shifting in this dynamic. The adult is the provider and the child is the seeker. Period.

By design, children come into the world seeking us. They actually cannot survive without some kind of physical *and* emotional connection to a capable, responding big person. The physical need for connectedness to big people is perhaps obvious—children need to be fed, watered, and sheltered in order to grow. But just as great as those physical needs is our children's need for an emotional connection that works well for the developing brain. As the emotional relationship solidifies, children become confident that their emotional needs are being provided for in a way that makes sense to their dependent self. And with this confidence that their big person can be counted on—that this person is an "expert," children are subconsciously freed to relax into their development.

Our job as caregivers is to become the "experts" for our children so that they are confident they can defer to us, comfortable and secure in our ability to lead, sort out, take care of, be in charge of, understand, and generally be intuitively guided by our incredible knowledge of their needs and concerns. Nobody knows our children better than we do, and nobody is more able to be their protector, to make sure their needs are met and their development unfolds exactly as nature intended.

DEPENDENCE & INDEPENDENCE

Often when I begin to talk about our children's need for dependence in their relationships with big people, big people start to get a little bit uncomfortable. There is something about the word "dependence" that gets people all up in arms. We have a very interesting pop culture around parenting, early childhood education, development in middle childhood and even into adolescence, whereby one of the core values that is championed as essential and important in growing up little people is *independence.* In other words, the belief is that our children need to *learn* to be independent, and that big people should not do for children what they can and should do for themselves. If they never *learn* to be independent, the thinking goes, how will they ever make it in this world?

If independence is where it is at, then the popular belief is that there is no better time than the present. Our children can't still have us carrying their backpacks into the classroom for them in Grade 12, so they best learn to do it by themselves now. They can't still be sleeping in our bed when they are sixteen, so they best become independent sleepers now. They are going to have to figure out how to pack themselves a lunch sooner or later, so they best get on it now. This hyperfocus on the apparent merits of learning independence is being applied to children at younger and younger ages, and in the face of this, it may seem odd for me to be encouraging big people to engage with children in a manner that promotes dependence rather than independence. The rub comes in understanding how a child develops independence.

To a certain extent, it is true that children really do require experiences that allow them to spread their wings a bit and see where they land. In having these experiences, they will of course gain confidence in their ability to do things on their own. However, when we think about what true independence is, it is when children really earnestly *desire* to spread their wings and try. Not when they are forced to "learn" it by their big people. Dependence is a necessary part of developing true independence because it provides the security and rest necessary for child development to naturally unfold.

Let me give you an example. When our youngest son, Maxwell, was in kindergarten, he was a blundering hot mess—or, in other words, a completely typical sensitive 5-year-old—when it came to getting him into his classroom each morning. It was hard for him to be up so early, and he often lamented how long his school day was. He was generally a bit disregulated, needing lots of connection, reassurance, and support from his big people to get settled. As a result, I encouraged a lot of dependence each morning. I spent extra time with him before we left the house. I carried his bag for him most days. I did his shoes up for him most days. I helped him into and out of his jacket most days. I definitely packed his bag for him every day. A lot of days I also unpacked his bag when we arrived at school. And I, by and large, supported him in his state of being an organizational jellyfish because I knew *that was what he needed*. He needed to be dependent on me because the school day kicked up for him a whole lot of unsettled feelings. And in intuitively understanding that for him, I was literally moved on his behalf to respond by encouraging dependence. Deep inside I knew that in allowing him to hold on to me that way, I would grant him some reprieve from all the things that caused him stress, which would help him to become more regulated. "Independence in the morning routine" is often touted as a key developmental milestone for kindergarten-aged students. So I am pretty sure that others noticed my encouragement of Maxwell's dependence, and may have even disapproved. But this was what Maxwell needed. How did I know? Not because I am a psychologist who works with children, but because I am Maxwell's mom and I know him. It wasn't something I planned in advance, but my instinctive heart understood that this was what was required.

Fast forward a couple of years to the writing of this book, and Maxwell is now in Grade 2. I can say with great confidence that if I were to grab his bag for him out of the car before school, head on into the school building, and begin to unload it for him, he would wonder what was happening. He would think it strange. He would almost certainly tell me that he wants to carry his bag himself. He might even ask me to stop. It is only on a very, very rare day that his mom carrying his bag would actually go down well. These are the days when something is amiss—maybe he is getting sick or had a bad night's sleep or just got back from a vacation that threw off his routine—and the disregulation has settled back in. And on those rare mornings, you will still find me quietly encouraging his dependence once again.

Has Maxwell become way more independent in his morning routines than he was in kindergarten? Yes, *much!* Now ask yourself, is it because he *learned* this or does this happen for Maxwell now because he *desires* it? Clearly in wanting to carry his own bag now, he desires it. In allowing Maxwell to be dependent on me early on, I laid the foundation for this desire to carry his own bag and a whole host of other "independent" actions to emerge from somewhere deep inside, such that he is now tidily and happily independent most mornings.

What would have happened had I insisted that Maxwell *learn* to be independent in kindergarten when he so clearly needed me? What if I had said to him, "Maxwell, you are a big boy now. Mommies don't carry backpacks for 5-year-olds. You need to carry this bag yourself." Or "Maxwell, you are a 5-year-old big boy and you need to tie your shoes yourself—end of story!" Do you think that today Maxwell would be happily engaging in his morning routine with relative independence? While he might be following through on the orders to "learn or else," I can assure you that it would not be from a place of desire or with a happy heart. He would be doing so grudgingly. It is true that some of the other children in Maxwell's kindergarten class appeared to be significantly more independent in their morning routines, but I cannot help but wonder whether it emanated from a fear of disapproval or from authentic desire.

The *appearance* of independence is not the same thing as the *development* of independence. Children learn how to mimic, and they create behavioral façades quite easily, especially if these come with approval—that is, "connection"—from their big people. But true independence is not something that can be copied so easily; it is acquired slowly and certainly as intuitive big people masterfully provide what they sense their children need and champion their children's dependence on us, no matter what. In gifting our children the opportunity to be deeply dependent on us, we also gift them the possibility of becoming people who desire to *do* and to *become,* in other words possessed of an independence that comes from somewhere deep inside.

☛ Give them some space

Many times when I speak publicly about the independence-dependence dynamic, I get asked about "helicopter parenting." This is the kind of parenting style in which parents hover over their children, seeing to their every need and protecting them from all manner of hurts and disappointments. The concern seems to be that if you are facilitating all of this dependence, are you not doing your children a disservice and even robbing them of opportunities to develop confidence? Of course you would be doing them a disservice! The intrusiveness that comes with helicopter parenting is very unsettling for children. Usually it is born of a parent's fears and insecurities, which soon become the child's own fears and insecurities.

Do not mistake a big person's insecure presence (the hoverer) with a caregiver's assured invitation of dependence (the provider). The hoverer is worried, nervous, and uncertain. The provider is confident, all-knowing, and in charge. The hoverer's actions are born of fear. The provider's actions—including the invitation for dependence—are born of confidence in knowing the needs of the child. Thus, on that fateful day when a child's desire bubbles forth and she says, "I want to carry my own backpack today," the responses will be very different. The hovering big person might say: "No, no, Mommy can do this. There, there, don't you fuss yourself about that..." In contrast, the providing big person, intuitively understanding the child's *desire* for independence, is going to reply: "Of course you want to carry your own backpack. Let me hand it to you!"

HULKING IT UP

I like to refer to the very in-charge "position" of the big person as the "Hulk" position—a reference to the fact that nobody would ever question the capable authority of the Incredible Hulk. When big people are "hulking it up," their "ways of being" are like the incredibly powerful, unwavering, and unquestionable presence of the Marvel Comics superhero when he is in full-on Hulk mode. But unlike the Hulk, big people who are hulking it up do so in more subtle ways. They are capably and confidently handling whatever needs to be handled with quiet, assured, consistent actions that are full of compassion, care, nurturance, and understanding. In the eyes of their children, big people who are hulking it up are efficient, on-top-of-it rock stars that have their children's needs front and center. A wonderful parent support program called "Circle of Security"[1] explains, "Your children need you to be bigger, stronger, wiser, and kind," and it is exactly this flavor that hulking it up for your children needs to embody.

Big people often get confused about what hulking it up looks like. By way of explanation, consider Richard. A couple of years ago I began a new fitness program that uses boxing and kickboxing as a form of exercise. As I sweat it out at the gym, several wonderful trainers there call out encouragement, offer tips, invite me to hang in for just another minute as I gasp for air. But none of them quite hulks it up like Richard, who co-owns the facility with his wife. When Richard swaggers in, everyone becomes a little more focused, works a little harder, throws in that extra bit of force. There is never a workout quite as intense as when he is in the house! And it is not because he is yelly-shouty, demanding, fierce, or scary. In fact, he is very kind and very understanding. But he is certain. He is certain of what it is you need, certain of how this should look, and certain of his ability to make you reach better, stronger, bigger outcomes.

The key is in *how* Richard conveys that certainty. He doesn't hammer it in with a flouting of knowledge and expertise. He doesn't hammer it in with belittling comments. And he doesn't hammer it in with forced authority. Instead, his certainty is conveyed in how tall he stands, how quietly he provides instruction, how confidently he calls out a command. He knows that even if he turns his back to pace across the room, you will execute without question. It is his unwavering belief in his expertise and ability to use that for our betterment—his quiet, efficient, and inherent conviction. He just is and he just does. Before and after a session on his gym floor, he takes time to connect with people, asking after their children, their partners, their jobs, their lives. He suggests movies and books that he thinks relate to something about what you have shared with him. And as you depart, sweaty and exhausted, he invites you to have a great day and often has a comment about seeing you again soon. He simply knows you will be back. Richard hulks it up without giving it a thought. He comes at this quiet confidence from a very natural, intuitive, organic place, and definitely by building a relationship with each of his trainees. And as a result, those of us on the gym floor are subconsciously and mechanistically compelled to be our best when he is present. We have found a position of *dependence* with this trainer because we believe in most everything he puts out into the space between him and us.

Our children need this same kind of hulking-it-up swagger from us. Their inborn dependence upon us means they are naturally looking towards us to guide them. We are meant to be IT for them! So imagine what it must feel like when they look to us for emotional and physical support and see that we have lost our swagger, or maybe never had it on in the first place. It might be that sigh of frustration. It might be that exasperated "I don't know what to do with you anymore!" It might be the tears that overtake us during an impossibly difficult day. Whatever the case, these non-Hulk moments are frightening to children. This is not surprising. If the trainer at my gym were to mope around the floor or shout that I am beyond hope or roll his eyes about my incorrect technique, I would very quickly deflate. I would no longer feel inspired to be there. I would dread going, and I would probably stay in my warm, cozy bed on the mornings when it felt difficult to get to the gym. The same thing happens for our children. If they experience us as having lost our swagger too often and/or for long periods of time, they deflate and lose their inspiration too.

☛ Bonding versus binding

One of the most important characteristics of big people who are adept at being ultimately and lovingly in charge for their little people is that they work within the nurturing nest of that relationship so that the full force of their swagger lands with the desired message. Amongst the reasons my trainer is so effective is that he works within relationship: he has forged bonds with the members of his gym by cultivating trust and by taking the time to connect about books and movies and goals before and after workouts. It is because of the bonded nature of the relationship that the members find themselves mechanistically responding to his swagger. It isn't just that he is a trainer. It is that he is a trainer *with heart* who builds relationships with his trainees and uses the natural power that creates to pull out of his trainees their very best performance.

Imagine instead that this trainer was very yelly-shouty and belittling, that he didn't take the time to create relationships. There is some power in that kind of a presence, but it is a power fueled by fear rather than a power emanating from relationship. It is the difference between *bonding* within the nurturing nest of *relationship* and *binding* within the context of established *roles*. Binding is created by nothing other than circumstance. For example, "I am your mother and because you were born to me, we are bound together. And because in this binding I am the big person, you will do as I say." Bonding is created by relationship cultivated through enduring experience. In other words, "I am your mother, and I adore you. I will always take care of you and have your best interests at heart." Or, to go back to my example of the trainer, "You will do this because I own this place and that is what I told you to do!" comes from a "bind" kind of place. This is a prescribed circumstance of him as the owner of the gym and me as the trainee. In the "bond" kind of gym he currently runs, where he has the power of relationship working for him, all he has to do is walk behind someone and quietly but firmly say: "Hit from the core!" and every core muscle in that person will engage to hit harder and stronger. His power comes from his connection with people *and* from hulking it up. It turns out that these are exactly the same two key things that children need to be naturally and fully dependent on their big people.

CONNECTION. As discussed in chapter 2, connection is the foundation of healthy child development. Children must have connection within a healthy big person–child relationship, and adults require the natural power that comes from this relationship to safely guide children through life.

HULK SWAGGER. Relationship without hulk swagger is not enough. Children need to believe that their big people are capable of growing them up so they can simply rest into the dependent position in their relationship with these adults. Connection, care, and trust tinged by anxiety, fouled by frustration, or hijacked by insecurity force children to make certain their big people are doing their job properly. And these children are not able to rest until their intuitive need for guidance and leadership is met. And so they will seek it by getting into the driver's seat and taking charge. Through their behavior, children will make sure there is a response of some kind, will make sure you meet their need, will make sure they do not go without.

When children, instead of their big people, become the Hulk, a whole new beast is unleashed. Children are not able to settle into natural childhood growth and development, and they will often exhibit challenging, Hulk-related behaviors that can drain the energy right out of their big people.

THE CHILD AS HULK

I have already described how children come out of the womb looking for the eyes of a big person, and how big people are wired to respond to these efforts, with a blooming of love and affection in the moment those little eyes find ours. This connection allows for a very early, very intuitive unfolding of a child's dependence on special big people. The child needs us in order to grow, learn, and develop, and this need for us is so deep that if a child does not sense confidence in our ability to take care, respond, nurture, and hulk it up for her, she will *demand* it mechanistically by way of some very challenging behaviors.

Several significant problems come with a child who is trying to be in charge, one of the most damaging being that the child's efforts will always be in vain. A child that has had to demand that you step up and do your big person job can *never* be satisfied or brought to a state of restful confidence in you, no matter how spectacular your response. A colleague once shared a story that illustrates why this is so.

On her birthday, a woman spends the day musing about the different possibilities for how her husband might celebrate with her. She's yearn-ing for a special treat, and obviously he is planning a surprise as he has made no mention of dinner reservations, get-togethers with friends, or any other such engagement. Maybe they will go for dinner at the fancy new restaurant down at the beach, she thinks. Or maybe he will show up after work with flowers and takeout from the place they had their first date all those years ago. Who knows?! The day sparkles with possibilities. When her husband arrives home from work, she excitedly opens the front door to greet him. He says "hello," plants a quick kiss on her cheek, and sails by her into the powder room to wash his hands. Her heart falls.

"Ummmm, hello," she begins. She pauses slightly and then asks, "Was there something else you were going to say?" Her husband stares at her—dazed like a deer caught in the headlights—and it is clear that he is frantically scanning his brain for something he might have forgotten. His face suddenly lights up and he exclaims: "Happy Birthday, Sweetie!" By now, however, her heart is firmly in her stomach as it is clear he has genuinely forgotten, and she counters, "That's it? No flowers, nothing?! Just 'Happy birthday'?!" Keen to right his apparent wrong, the husband tells her to hang on just one second, as he races out the front door. She hears his car start up again and he is off. Ten minutes later, he returns, flowers in hand, and grandly presents them to her.

How do you suppose those flowers are received? The woman might say, "Oh, thanks. So nice of you to think of me," as she fumes that her husband has forgotten her special day and had to be prompted to mark the occasion in any way. And likely the rest of the evening (or longer!) will be colored by what has happened. No matter what the husband does at this point he will not be able to regain his wife's confidence. Why? Because she had to ask for it. Because in failing to be on top of it, understanding, sensitive, etc., he has presented himself as incapable, not in charge, not to be counted on.

This same dynamic plays out with children—only they will always be on the "receiving" end of the flowers. If they look around and find that their big people are not really understanding, do not move to take care accordingly, are not picking up what they are putting down, and generally just aren't getting it, those big people get demoted. Just as the husband raced out to get flowers in his demoted state, so too will we as big people hurry-scurry to make it right for our demanding, hulked-up children. And just as the woman will find little comfort in the flowers her husband eventually produces, our children will also find little comfort in our responsiveness when they have had to demand it because they cannot trust that we can and will deliver. And because they *need* responsiveness, *need* dependence on their big people, they cannot sit idly by and allow themselves to wither away. Like the woman in the story, they will demand flowers. And the demand for flowers can come in all sorts of interesting forms.

NEEDINESS. Some children will present as very "needy" in their hulked-up state. Existing in a persistent state of not being confident that their needs can be effectively met—including and perhaps most importantly their deepest emotional needs—has left them needing constant reassurance. This may mean a never-ending stream of anxious questions: How do you know that won't happen? How can you be sure? Or it may rear up as separation anxiety: your child cannot bear to be apart from you and must constantly hold on to you for dear life because somehow in his eyes you cannot be counted on to return. Or it may manifest at nighttime: your child cannot sleep unless he is directly snuggled up with you.

BOSSINESS. Some children in their hulked-up state will come across as bossy and demanding. Your child might order you around: "Talk to the hand, Mommy!" or "You do that, Daddy, because I said," or "Try and make me, Mrs. Jones. I dare you." Or your child might try to take charge of a situation that you or another big person should be in charge of; for example, doling out discipline to classmates.

EXTREME INDEPENDENCE. Other children will show a debilitating incapacity to surrender to dependence of any kind when in their hulked-up state. Your young child might not let you help her with anything, no matter that she is combusting with frustrated tears. Occasionally this inability to surrender to dependence can become very worrisome, particularly when it involves feeding. Children may refuse to be fed, may refuse any food that you have prepared, or may not be able to hold the food in their stomach. Older children might also blatantly lie or keep secrets about apparent shortcomings or faults, like a poor grade at school or a fallout with a friend or sibling, as talking about these would provoke an unsettling sense of too much dependence.

PRECOCIOUSNESS. When children come across as miniature adults it can be seen as "cute" or seem to indicate "confidence," but it may be a behavior associated with being in a hulked-up state. A YouTube video called *Linda, honey, just listen*, in which a 3-year-old boy confidently makes a case to his mother for why he really shouldn't be in trouble for eating cupcakes, recently went viral. The little boy in the video adeptly controls the conversation, using comments such as "Linda, honey, just listen . . . ," and doling out advice to Linda about how he and his brother should be managed. Not surprisingly, a lot of the comments in the feed are quite positive in nature: how smart, clever, well spoken, and confident this boy is. Indeed, many hulked-up children are misattributed these kind of traits at first glance. However, as I watched the video, I could not help but worry about the boy's tone and posturing, and why he finds himself in a position where he feels the need to catapult himself into the driver's seat and take charge.

PARENTING THE BIG PEOPLE. When they are in a hulked-up state, some children begin to take care of their big people. They act in ways that try to avoid upsetting their big people or they try to smooth over any physical or emotional hurts that might occur. For example, if you get injured, your child might tend to your wounds. Or if it looks as though you are about to lose a board game, your child might "let" you win so you don't feel bad. Your child may also avoid telling you about bad grades or try to patch up a conflict between big people or put on a sunshine-and-roses happy face, all in an effort to care for you as though you are not able to manage otherwise.

EXCESSIVE PERSISTENCE. And some children will show excessive persistence when they are in a hulked-up state. Your child might fall, slightly scrape her knee, but then scream and cry and erupt hysterically. Even when you respond with appropriate care and attention, she will continue to scream and cry, seemingly unable to be soothed. This is a different kind of "demanding" that typically involves children who experience a lot of ups and downs, and at times exist in an intensely disregulated state. It appears almost as though they are resisting dependence on their big person, that they are unable to trust whether that big person will meet the need and for how long.

Children who present with one or more of this constellation of behaviors are going to be exhausting to their big people. And furthermore, it will be almost impossible for the big people to be in charge, to guide or lead, and more generally to grow these children up. The child has become the Hulk. The child is in the driver's seat. In the same way that it was uncomfortable for the woman to accept the flowers she had demanded, it becomes very uncomfortable for the hulked-up child to accept offers of dependence and general care and leadership from big people. Hulked-up children desperately want and, in fact, *need* to be dependent on big people, but they cannot accept it from a big person who has lost their in-charge swagger.

For some children, these hulked-up behaviors will pop up here and there but are not really an enduring pattern. For other children, these behaviors are—or are on their way to becoming—deeply entrenched. The difference lies in whether or not a child's belief system classifies his big people as in charge (the Hulk) or incapable (dehulkified). Lots of children have strong personalities and a propensity for enjoying being in charge, being leaders, and the like. This in and of itself is not a concern. What is a concern is when a child *cannot* find herself in the dependent position with her big people. *Ever.*

I often ask big people to reflect on the last time they can remember their little person coming to them with a significant need, and especially coming to them with soft tears and vulnerability around that need. If you can pinpoint a situation recently in which your little person came to you with that kind of soft, vulnerable quest for dependence, but you still think he can be bossy and demanding at times, it is probably more a temperament thing. If, however, you are pressed to recall when your little person last came to you without hot, angry tears or other hard, hulked-up behaviors, your child may have stepped into the in-charge position. Perhaps you didn't have your hulk on enough or perhaps your child's needs are so significant they seem to have overwhelmed your capacity to provide for them.

☛ Regain your parental swagger

The reality of being demoted from the in-charge position often creeps up on big people. It typically isn't until the point at which the child's behaviors have so overwhelmed us that we realize the position we are in. The difficulty is that big person dehulkification is not a straight-forward, easily explained process. But there are 2 key variables in the dance between the big person and child that should be considered: the strength of the swagger and the needs of the child.

Your ability to hulk it up is key in arriving at the beautiful place of being able to gift your children dependence on you. If they experience you as generally uncertain, often unglued, or typically overwhelmed, then likely your hulk swagger is not what it needs to be. Consider what your barriers to swagger are and see what you can do to remove them. Maybe you need more support from people in your life—see how you can access that support. Maybe you need to reduce some of the stressors in your world—get after reducing them. Maybe you need to get on top of routine and consistency in your home to feel more settled—then make that happen. It is ultimately important that you find a way back, slowly but certainly, to having your swagger.

Your child's needs and intensity will determine just how present your swagger should be. Some children by design are going to be more settled and less intense. Other children will have personalities and temperaments that are more demanding. It goes without saying that the more intense the child, the more present your swagger will need to be. In addition, some children genuinely have greater need than other children. These include, but are not limited to, children who are emotionally sensitive, children who have sensory needs (with nervous systems that react intensely to incoming sensory inputs (sounds, tastes, smells, etc.)), children who struggle with regulation from a biological cause, children who have experienced significant hurts or wounds, children who have witnessed or experienced abuse, children who have experienced trauma of any kind, children who have been adopted and/or placed into foster care, and children whose parents have divorced. In many of these cases, the caring adults who are trying so hard to figure out the needs of their children will have to become utterly exceptional at being that in-charge, confident, capable big person. They will *have to be* exceptional at this because their children are exceptional and will demand it in order to come to rest in their care.

Big people who are solid, confident, in-charge guides leading their children through the up-and-down journey of growing and developing are *essential*. In chapters 6 and 7, I present some ideas for regaining your footing if you have lost your swagger. One of the most important things you or any big person can do to discipline without damage is to ensure you have your swagger on!

VULNERABILITY & GROWTH

Why is it so important that children are grown up by big people who know how to hulk it up? Nobody would disagree that children should be able to depend on their big people for physical protection, so why should the same not be true of emotional protection? And we just learned the essential benefit of inviting dependence to promote the emergence of true independence. There is another reason children need their bigger, wiser, and kinder hulked-up big people: the essential role of vulnerability in truly growing up.

Think back to the example of the medical clerk that we opened with in this chapter. Remember what happened when you caught her making that mistake? Remember how right away you felt a surge of anger and experienced a need to make sure she knew she had a) messed up and b) needed to fix it? Remember how you refused to acquiesce to her invitation to sit down and wait for your name to be called next, and instead you forced the issue by standing right beside her counter? Remember how the next time you went to that office you were much more demanding in ensuring that your needs were met by marching on up to her counter and announcing your spot in the lineup as being NEXT?!

If we were to pull apart that example, we would see several important themes emerge. For starters, you are definitely not in a relaxed state. It is clear that when you are around this person/this situation, you are expending a lot of energy trying to exact some control where you have experienced a lack of control. You are putting effort into being sure that you are understood, treated fairly, responded to appropriately, etc., and this is driving you to behave in ways that are probably experienced by the clerk as rude, bossy, interfering, and intense. Why are you acting this way? Recall that it was because of a mechanistic shift in your mindset about the clerk's capabilities—you no longer believed her to be effective in her role and so you felt you needed to take matters into your own hands. Our children, too, take matters into their own hands when they have had to demand care from us for their needs. And this makes them unable to relax into their development. They will always be on a quest.

They will never quite feel satiated in their need for dependence. They will always be making sure that their demands land with us in time. To be the kind of big person that our children need requires that we engage in relationship with them in a way that allows them to relax into the journey of growing up and developing on their own time.

Recently I came across a posting online that read as follows:

A little girl and her father were crossing a bridge.

The father was kind of scared so he asked his little daughter:

"Sweetheart, please hold my hand so that you don't fall into the river."

The little girl said:

"No, Dad. You hold my hand."

"What's the difference?" asked the puzzled father.

"There's a big difference," replied the little girl.

"If I hold your hand and something happens to me, chances are that I may let your hand go. But if you hold my hand, I know for sure that no matter what happens, you will never let my hand go."

In any relationship, the essence of trust is not in its bind, but in its bond. So hold the hand of the person whom you love rather than expecting them to hold yours...[2]

This short story illustrates the importance of children's trust in being able to depend on us. If they know that we've got it, we're on it, we're picking up what they are putting down, and we've got their backs, then they won't have to ask for it. They can just rely on it and redirect the energy they would otherwise have used for ensuring its provision to the things that children are meant to spend energy on.

This little story would have been utter perfection in demonstrating how to hulk it up if the dad had said, "I am going to hold your hand," so that his daughter did not have to ask for it. And if he had not had to ask "why" or experience "puzzlement," because he "just knew." And in just knowing, he would have given his daughter the opportunity to trust in her dependence on him. In the brilliant words of Dr. Gordon Neufeld, "We need to hold on, so they can let go." Children are not free to grow, learn, and develop as nature intended if they have to pour energy into ensuring their need for us is taken care of, even if it means their own growth is stunted.

Think back again to the medical clerk and the themes we pulled out of our hypothetical but highly probable reaction to her. Our children respond the same way if they experience us as not really being in charge. They no longer look to us for solace; instead, they look to see if we are doing it right. And doing this leaves them unable to relax into dependence because they are constantly having to police whether we are seeing and meeting their needs or whether they need to ask for our help or seek it another way. They need our nurturing care and connection, but when they have to ask for it, the need automatically becomes impossible to meet.

Children stuck in this kind of a dynamic start to find that they cannot depend, even when a ripe opportunity or an actual need presents. Even in times of extreme sadness, fear, or other upset, they cannot count on solace. And this is a very frightening place for the mind to be. To protect itself, the human psyche is wired to resist the persistence of this frightened state. If it goes on too long and/or occurs too often, a series of neurological and emotional reactions unfold to provide the mind with some rest from the distress. Psychologists called this process *dissociation*, which means that the mind tunes out the upsetting things around it. Although this transformation is remarkable in what it suggests about the human brain's capacity for adaptability and neuroplasticity, the need to tune out is devastating when considered in the context of development.

Children need to feel in order to grow. They must be able to experience something upsetting like disappointment to then experience what it is to grieve and recover, developing resilience along the way. And yet in the absence of a sense of safety and dependence in the presence of their big people, children will become highly distressed and turn off their feelings to avoid the ongoing hurt whenever their true needs are not met. In other words, when children feel too vulnerable to bring forward their hurts and upsets, their mind protects them but these hurts and needs go unaddressed and fester. Neurologist and psychoanalyst Sigmund Freud is reputed to have said that unexpressed emotions never die. They just come forth later in uglier ways. And this is true of children who have turned off their feeling self. Those pushed-down emotions resurface as anxiety, anger, frustration, and all matter of big, ugly feelings. And children who lack the capacity to present their needs in a vulnerable way to their big people cannot know dependence, and in not knowing dependence they will never know true independence. And thus, for a child who has met with such a fate, life becomes a state of persistent immaturity, incapacity for resilience, and lack of energy to direct towards the joys of growing.

☛ *Believe & be good enough*

Sometimes the enormity of our responsibility to growing children up in the best possible way can seem alarming. We can begin to drown in the "what if's?" or the "how could I have's?" or the "why did I's?" or the "is it enough's?" With these thought patterns bashing about in our big people heads, it is no wonder that guilt not only sets in but threatens to undo us at times. And yet, as we have talked at length about in this chapter, hulking it up and having your swagger on and being that all-knowing-in-charge-game-on-nurturing kind of big person is of central importance. How exactly do we do this if we are drowning in worry about whether or not we are doing a good job?

There are 2 key ideas that all big people can hold on to when faced with guilt and uncertainty about growing up their children: 1) you only need to be *good enough* and 2) you need to find your belief in yourself.

I am a psychologist who has spent her academic and professional life studying and supporting children and parents. As a result, it might make sense that I know a few things about what children need. But I promise you that had you been a fly on the wall in my house most any week, you would have seen me drop the ball! I would have had a harsh word for one of my children, become frustrated at our late departure for school, or grumped about how messy the entryway is. I am not a perfect parent. I mess it up. All the time. Sometimes I even get on a roll with messing things up because I have become too stressed or allowed my workload to get away from me. Why does this happen, even when my life's work is devoted to knowing what is best for children? Because that is what it is to be human. But I know 2 things for sure—I am good enough and I believe in myself as a big person. And that is all it takes. You have to know for yourself that you are good enough and you have to believe that you've got this.

BEING GOOD ENOUGH. The developmental literature actually coined this phrase to convey the message that children do not need us to be perfect.[3] They simply need us to be good enough. What is good enough? Well, it is different for every child, but generally speaking, if most of the time you hulk it up, swagger about, and encourage dependence, all in a nurturing, compassionate manner, you are going to be good enough. In telling us that we don't have to be perfect, developmental science has also given us the message that we need to be very gentle with ourselves around the guilt that we might feel. I encourage every big person to hold on to just a little bit of that guilt and allow it to motivate you to do and be better. But let the rest go. You need only be good enough, and according to your child, good enough is spectacular.

BELIEVING IN YOURSELF. Beyond holding on to the idea that I am good enough for my children, I truly believe that I am the answer for them. I believe to the core of my being that I know their hearts and their souls, so I am their ultimate big person. Even in situations where I may not be sure about exactly what is eating away at our 11-year-old or why our 8-year-old has been so upset of late, or what to do about that problem at school or that medical issue or a zillion other things, I really and truly believe that I can rock it out for them. Sometimes I will fake my way through situations until I make it, but even then I know I am it for them. The key is all about that hulk swagger. Similarly, a lot of times the single most important role I play for my clients is to nurture their belief in themselves, and the vast majority of these big people will find their stride. As soon as they begin to see themselves as the child's answer, to recognize that nature set us up to step into that place of being this lovingly in-charge, caring big person to the child, then there is no limit to what they can do for their children.

If you have a child with significant needs, for whom the world is a hard place to exist, you might find yourself constantly working at being bigger than his need and you might often feel like your child's behavior does not appear to indicate that your efforts are taking root. But keep the faith. You must trust that you are impacting his development in a very profound way. You are sculpting neural circuitry that is going to eventually allow him to regulate more effectively. You are cultivating belief systems that will stand him in good stead as he faces life's challenges. If not right now or even if not anytime soon, eventually you will see how staying the course and championing your child's developmental needs above all else is the ticket.

If you are the answer for your children, does this then mean you are also the problem? No! That is not at all what it means. Certainly, there are circumstances where big people have done wrong by children in awful ways. In those situations, big people are to be held accountable for that harm. But for the vast majority of big people, the child's challenges were not intentionally caused by a big person. Big people genuinely want the best for their children. Just because you weren't necessarily the cause of a little person's challenges does not mean you are not the answer. You *are* the answer. Your "good enough" is magnificent to your children. Your belief in yourself to BE it for them is utterly empowering for them. And your generosity in gifting them the opportunity to be deeply dependent on you as you lead the way alters your children's life course forever. Imagine that finding our way through and doing right by our children could be so simple!

THE LETTER NO CHILD SHOULD
EVER HAVE TO WRITE

Much of my work with parents and other big people is centered on having the big person really and truly see the world through a child's eyes. It is my belief that if big people can do this in an enduring way, it allows us very intuitively to shift our way of being with our children. We see their needs in a new light. We see our role in a new light. We see discipline in a new light. And so, to really walk you into the mind of a child and have you truly experience discipline through those eyes, I invite you to read the letter that no child should ever have to write.

Dear Big Person of Mine,
From that first moment I was born, as soon as I could get my little eyes open, I looked all around until I found your eyes. And when I found them, I stared into them with intensity because I knew right from the start that you were my best bet. I knew that I needed you more than anything or anyone else to be

able to survive and thrive in this life I had been born to. I knew that I would need to hang on to you and be protected and shielded by your safe embrace to even have a chance at riding out the physical and emotional challenges I would face in my life ahead. I knew all of this, even though I did not yet know my name, your name, or anything else about who I was. This was nature's way of ensuring that the ingredients necessary to my safe upbringing were immediately in play.

It seemed to go pretty well that first year. There was a lot of rocking and holding and smiling and shushing and all the things that had me feeling really safe and settled. Where it kind of seemed to go sideways for me was that day when I was 2 and a bit, and I really, really, really wanted that stuffy at the store. Do you remember that day? I was a bit tired, having missed a nap to get the shopping done. And I spied that stuffy out of the corner of my eye. It looked soft and snuggly, and I thought it would be heaven to sink my tired little head into it while I waited for you to finish shopping. But you didn't know how much I needed it, so you said no. I was super sad. And my sad blew up into this crazy kind of mad. I felt really out of control. I couldn't stop it. The yells and the kicks and the hits were just flying out of me. I wanted to stop but my brain had already lost it. There was no turning back. It just needed to run its course.

Unfortunately, this was right after you had read that book about discipline. That book told you that adults needed to be in charge and that children were never to think they had got away with something. That if you let them think this, they would soon believe they ruled the roost and you would lose all control of them. The book also told you that the best way to sort me out was to give me some "quiet time." And that it was best if you made that quiet time be something that I wouldn't really love, just in case that made me have more meltdowns in order to get more quiet time. So the book told you to make the quiet time be me on my own somewhere quiet, without any potential "rewards" like toys... or even like you nearby. And to have the quiet time end only when I had stopped my meltdown.

So when I got really upset about not getting the stuffy, that is what you did. You took me out of the shopping cart and found a quiet spot in the store where you sat me down and told me to calm down. You said that I could be done sitting there once I was calm. I didn't know what to do. My brain was going crazy with mad and now my heart was going crazy with sad. I saw you walk away. You—my best bet, my only bet, the one I need more than anything or anyone else to be able to survive this life—and you were walking away at a time when I really needed you to help me. I looked around wildly, trying to see if there was someone or something else—like maybe I could substitute that stuffy if it was somewhere nearby. I mean, it wouldn't have been anything like you, but I was desperate to find something. And quickly I realized there was nothing. I wanted you back so badly. I was really scared.

And then this super-weird thing happened. My crazy brain went quiet. It did not go calm; it just went quiet. In needing you back so badly, it went quiet so that I could get you back. Because you said that if I stopped crying and fussing, the quiet time would be over, which would mean I would get you back! And I guess my brain knew that you were the priority. So I stuffed the tears and sad and mad and crazy away. And I looked up to see where you were. You were standing a little way away from me with your back to me (I think the book had also told you not to give me any attention while I carried on). I wished you had been looking at me then so you could have seen that I needed you. It would have been so amazing in that moment if you had realized that this wasn't working and had rushed over and scooped me up and let me know you had me—that you were the kind of best bet that could be counted on. But you weren't looking.

I stuffed down a few more tears. And then I toddled on over to where you were standing. You told me "good job" for stopping and then told me that was not acceptable behavior and that next time you expected I would not cry just because you weren't getting me what I wanted. You told me that adults call those the "greedy gimmees" and that it is not a nice thing for kids to do.

I swallowed some more tears. I wondered how you could not see that it was just a soft-looking stuffy and I was tired. That's all.

I think that is the moment where it all started—me wondering if you were the kind of best bet that could be counted on or the kind of best bet that had to be earned. Of course, life carried on and I grew taller and smarter and went about the business of all the things kids are supposed to do, like making friends and going to school and playing soccer. But I wish you could have known what happened inside of me every single time you sent me away from you to calm down. Or took away from me something I loved so that you could get out of me something you wanted. Or put up a star chart, which would always have me so panicked about not getting a star that I worked harder than I had ever worked before. I wish you could have known. I wish you could know now.

Really all I ever needed was for you to react in those moments with kindness. I just needed to be calmed. It would have been okay for me not to get the stuffy or whatever it was that the "no" was about, as long as I had you. I would have figured out sooner or later how it goes in a store when you ask for something you don't need. And initially, maybe even for a few years, I may have been sad or mad for a little while when given a "no," but if you could have just held me—in your arms or with your voice or even with your eyes—it would have changed so much for me. I needed you to be my unquestionable best bet. I wish I could have had that sense that, no matter what, you were always going to deliver on that. I just needed you. I will always just need you. That's all. You.

Love,

Your Child

II

CONNECTION
IN ACTION

MAKING IT REAL

A speaker who was billed as an "expert" recently visited my children's school to deliver a presentation to the big people in our community on a topic related to parenting. I was unable to attend, but the next day many of my friends who had been there approached me full of excitement about all they had learned: the highlight being that parents should never come to the rescue of their children because children need to experience failure in order to mature. While I believe it *is* true that a child who never has the experience of facing disappointment and having to find a different way through will be hard-pressed in adulthood to manage the inevitable ups and downs of life, it is *not* true that parents should *never* come to the rescue of their children. The challenge with this sort of specific "how-to" strategy is that it presumes there's a one-size-fits-all idea that works with every child and in every circumstance.

What if your child is having a terrible day because of something that happened at home the night before? On this day does it still make sense not to come to her rescue? What if your child is highly sensitive and experiences failures, especially more significant ones, with a lot of intensity? Should you still not come to her rescue? What if your child is sick, tired, overwhelmed by school stress, or having learning challenges? Consider even the simplest application of that advice: what if your child fell in the playground and, as a result, was in physical distress? Would you not come to his rescue? Why should it be any different when your child is in emotional distress? Are you really not supposed to come to a child's rescue, *ever*? Even if it is something as small as delivering a forgotten lunch bag on a day that is already proving overwhelming to your child?

Perhaps the speaker had not intended to leave the audience with this take-home message. However, in offering a concrete strategy, the inevitable happened: big people, anxious for information about how to "do it right," grabbed on to what they saw as the quick fix. For many parents that evening, this strategy came across as universally applicable. When we start to apply a "rule" rather than using our knowledge of our children, our intuition, and our own judgment to make appropriate context-based decisions, the heart goes right out of the equation.

Big people often tell me they are confounded by how something can work so well with their child one day and be a giant, disastrous failure the next. Or how what works with one child is useless for his sibling. But why should it be the same for every child? Each child is a unique person from moment to moment, day to day, month to month, and year to year. In fact, we all are. Routinized, scripted, concrete strategies proffered as options for parents and other big people to manage the needs of their children have no heart. By "no heart," I mean there is no deep understanding of *that* child's needs in *that* moment on *that* day in *that* situation—there is no instinct. And without heart, the chosen strategy runs the risk of causing damage to the relationship between the big person and the child, *and* creating moments of disregulation in the child's brain.

If repeated too often or administered too intensely, strategies that are not informed by the intuitive heart of a big person can actually change the neurological wiring of a child's regulatory control center in the brain and alter important components of socio-emotional growth and development, including self-esteem and self-concept.[1] Developmental science offers very compelling evidence that all of this, in turn, leads a child to become significantly more vulnerable to developing anxiety, depression, and other mood-related difficulties in adolescence and/or adulthood, and to having a greater propensity for generally being disregulated, easily agitated, and attentionally challenged.

PARENTING WITH HEART

How, then, are big people supposed to grow up our children? Should we take everything we have ever learned from "experts" and toss it out of our minds? If we simply love our children enough, will they turn out okay? The answer is neither of these! To find our way through, the answer is always to go to the heart of the matter. If you can *see* your children's behavior, *feel* what is happening for them in that moment, and, as a result of feeling their hearts, *be* what it is they need you to be, you will be well on your way. By using this mantra to guide how you respond to your children's needs, no prescribed strategies are necessary. This is the start to discipline informed by heart.

THE 3 INTUITIVE COMPONENTS TO DISCIPLINE WITHOUT DAMAGE

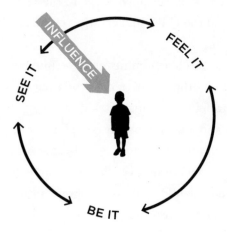

When big people take the time to see the behavior, what we need to understand most of all is that children's emotional and developmental needs are concealed below the surface. They are not visible but must be intuited. To really appreciate the depths of our child's needs, we must feel for them with a conscious awareness and compassion. There are no guarantees about what we will find there and there may be few, if any, patterns in this compassionate observation. Every child and situation is unique, and both can shift in an instant. A child's activated brain needs to be settled and regulated, and the big person's connection-informed responses to a child's behavioral cuing—"the regulatory dance"—are needed to gently lull the brain back to a more calm state.

When our compassionate feeling for our children is awakened within us, our intuition is able to come alive, and the necessary actions follow as we hold them safe and secure and be it alongside and for them. In "being it" for our children, we become the model of the kind of person we dream of them becoming when they grow up. We need to act on our certainty in understanding them, we need them to have confidence in our ability and willingness to act on this knowledge, and then we need to deliver. We need to *be*. Be in charge, be intuitive, be the big person. It is in all of these ways that we influence the development of our growing children: we see their behavior, we feel their needs, and we be what they need us to be. And all of this goes down between a big person and a child within the power of relationship. Relationship awakens intuition. Relationship stirs compassion. Relationship allows us to deliver. Relationship is the key to "being it" for our children.

Many clients I have worked with over the years would tell you their greatest struggle was knowing how to "be it" for their children, and further, lacking confidence in their ability to deliver on this. That is what *they* would tell you their greatest struggle was. I, however, entered into every one of those client relationships knowing that they had it in them. It is just the way we are.

Thinking about the relationship big people have with little people as embodying the characteristics of a dance—the "regulatory dance"— allows us to understand how being it comes alive for big people. When you are a beginner dancer, you learn a dance by memorizing footwork in a laborious and mechanical kind of way. You count beats. You look down at your feet. You stumble. You try again. But soon, you find your feet just starting to move without even thinking about it. You find different dance positions flowing out of you as if you'd always known how to do them. These natural rhythms and impulses play out without any conscious thought or intention. If you are a big person who worries that you might not have what it takes to "be it" for your child, hear me now... YOU DO!

Initially you may feel like you are analyzing every single situation and trying to piece together specific strategies and ideas. And that is fine. And it is also fine if you think you are stumbling along and not making a lot of progress at first. As you focus on building your relationship with your child, your intuition will sharpen, your compassion will deepen, and your ability to truly meet the needs of your child and champion his development will flourish exponentially. As author Dr. Wayne Dyer said, "I am a human being, not a human doing. Don't equate your self-worth with how well you do things in life. You aren't what you do. If you are what you do, then when you don't... you aren't."[2] We are not human *doings*; we are human *beings*. Discipline is not about what you do as much as it is about *being* for children what they need big people to be, and your actions, just like dancing, flow naturally from that. You've got this. No, *really*. You do. And if you need some help with fumbling your way through a few of those early dance steps until you feel like your heart and your intuition are alive and attuned to your child, no problem. I have some ideas to see you through to that day when you will pause and think, "Wow, I really do have this." And in that moment, know that I am nodding along with you. Because you *already* have this; you just need to allow it to be.

GET TO KNOW YOUR CHILD

To understand your child's needs in any specific moment, you also have to have a picture of her overall needs. It's like getting to know your dance partner: her strengths and challenges, favorite steps, and secret wishes. Having a sense of where your child, in all of her brilliant uniqueness, is on her own personal spectrum of needs at any given time is absolutely essential to informing your intuition about how and when to respond. Without having a sense of a child's general level of need, you run the risk of charging in too quickly, of not providing a big enough safety net, or of generally responding in a way that worsens, rather than improves, the situation. As you focus on sharpening your intuition, you will have to be aware of *who* your child is, *how* she ticks, *what* works for her (and what definitely does not), and more generally, knowing where your child is at and what is required from you in response. In essence, you need a built-in "needs barometer" for your child.

☛ Assessing need using the "needs barometer"

All human beings encounter struggles, and it is normal to have some kind of reaction to these challenges. With children, the reactions are often bigger because their regulatory systems are still developing and they are not able to cope as well as adults are. They might be tired or hungry, they might have a grouchy teacher, or they might be stressed about the upcoming soccer tournament. Since each child is unique in terms of temperament, developmental patterns, and general emotional makeup, the responses to these situations may be different. It doesn't mean something is wrong with the child or with you. It just means that the more intense the need, the greater the demand for sharpened intuition and heart so you can be for your child exactly what it is that he truly needs from you. For example, following a disappointing loss in a soccer game or during a visit to a loud, busy playground, a child who by nature is very zen will have a different level of need than a child who by nature is very emotionally sensitive. It isn't about what is normal and not normal for any child, but about knowing the child you are growing up and ensuring that your knowledge of that child informs how you "be it" for him.

As life gets busy, you must sometimes stop and measure the intensity of a child's needs. I refer to this as taking their pressure on the needs barometer. Having a sense of your child's needs as you consider the bigger picture will help you know when to move in swiftly to help your child move on or when to hold steady, provide support, and push forward when your child's needs have been addressed. Consider the following specific needs and which levels might be becoming more intense or less intense on your child's needs barometer.

CHANGE. Children who have experienced and/or are experiencing one or more changes in their world will necessarily shift energy towards adapting to the new reality, which means less available energy for regulating around some of the ups and downs that are naturally part of everyday life. Change that can cause a significant surge of need in a child can be positive or negative, and can include moving to a new school, classroom, daycare, home, or neighborhood; getting used to a new teacher, sibling, blended family, or parenting figure (from remarriage/dating); or any other departure from what the child knows as comfortable and routine.

SHIFTS IN CONNECTION. Children who have experienced changes involving the nature of the relationship they have with the special big people to whom they are most intensely connected may have a higher level of challenge with internal regulation and managing the demands of a typical day. Such changes might include, but are not limited to, divorce, adoption, teacher changes, and changes in educational support personnel (e.g., special education assistants). The death of a special big person will also prompt a major shift in connection. It can take many years for children to incorporate significant shifts in their connections with those to whom they are most deeply connected.

EMOTIONAL SENSITIVITY. Some children naturally have a higher level of awareness of their own emotions and the emotions of those around them. When responded to by big people who are generally kind and nurturing, these children go on to become adults who are highly adept at social interaction and/or reading and understanding social engagement. Emotionally sensitive children often have challenges with self-control, especially when a situation has become intense for them. Just surviving a normal day can suck dry their energy reserves for emotional regulation as they hyperanalyze every look from their teacher for hints of approval or disapproval, consider every change in their parent's tone of voice to try to discern that parent's mood in any moment, and examine every snicker from a peer to determine if it was mocking or jovial.

NEUROLOGICAL SENSITIVITY. Some people, including children, experience the physical world day in and day out in a very intense way. Among other things, they might be acutely aware of smells (of people, the outdoors, food), sights (bright lights), sounds (constant background noise, certain kinds of movement), textures (seams in socks, tags in shirts, certain fabrics, etc.), tastes (too bitter, too sour, too harsh, etc.), and other experiences of the physical world that land intensely and divert a lot of children's energy to managing their own regulatory state. As a result, they may more quickly become disregulated, exhibit different kinds of challenging behaviors, and/or have trouble responding to boundaries that have been set for them, managing disappointments, and dealing with other concerns.

LOSS OF CONNECTION. Children who have experienced any form of loss may have a very diminished supply of coping reserves for navigating upsets and disappointments. Loss might include death (of a pet, family member, friend) or a pattern of disappointments or difficult realities (grandma moved away, mom is working extra long hours, and they didn't make the soccer team—all around the same time). Regardless of its origin, children who have experienced loss are likely to have a higher level of need.

EMOTIONAL NEGLECT. Children whose emotional needs have not been understood and championed by their special big people are at risk for having significant difficulties with regulation and managing upset. Children who have been removed from abusive homes and are in the protective care of a government agency may show signs of extreme emotional neglect. More subtle, although still extremely impactful, is the emotional neglect experienced by children whose big people might be unavailable to them too frequently and too intensely due to mental health and addiction issues or to the significant demands of an overwhelming professional life.

LEARNING EXCEPTIONALITIES. By definition, children with learning exceptionalities (also called disabilities) have average to higher levels of intelligence and are, by comparison, unable to actualize this intellect into performance with school-related learning (math, reading, writing, etc.). These children often have amazing gifts but learn differently from their peers and do not progress as quickly at school in a traditional learning environment. Since they are aware of their smarts yet utterly frustrated by how these smarts do not translate into strong classroom performance, children with learning exceptionalities typically carry enduring experiences of shame, frustration, and disappointment. As a result, they tend to be much more vulnerable to emotional upset and related behavioral difficulties.

DEVELOPMENTAL EXCEPTIONALITIES. Children growing up with developmental exceptionalities (or following a unique course of development as a result of autism, Down's syndrome, fetal alcohol spectrum disorder, developmental coordination disorder, etc.) may face a world full of physical, social, and emotional challenges that are inherent to their developmental profile. These are often exacerbated by the broader cultural context of exclusion and/or judgment from the people and institutions in the world around them. Ongoing experiences of frustration and upset can steal energy and regulatory resources away from these children's ability to cope with the normal ups and downs of a typical day.

STRESS. Children today cope with a lot more stress than the children of even one generation ago. They experience intense expectations around school and other kinds of performance (athletic, artistic) and/or they are often hyperscheduled. Children who experience stress daily and who do not have enough opportunity for emotional and physical rest are more susceptible to disregulation and behavioral challenges. Children existing in this kind of a daily reality also have a higher level of need for understanding and support than other children.

Regardless of the specific origin of a child's higher level of need, one thing is certain: if you have the responsibility of growing up an exceptional child with exceptional need, you must be an exceptional big person who is adeptly attuned to the needs of that child and can genuinely feel the child's internal reality and respond accordingly. See chapter 8 for more discussion about the specific needs of children with special circumstances surrounding their growth and development.

MATCH YOUR RESPONSE TO THE LEVEL OF NEED

Just as there is no set list of steps that tells big people exactly how to "do" discipline for each child, there is no set way to know how a child needs you to be and where you should begin. Are you growing up a child who right now is really struggling? Are you growing up a child who right now actually seems to be doing quite well emotionally? Are you growing up a child who has just come through a significant and challenging life event and appears to be okay but may be wondering when the other shoe will drop? When engaging in ways of being for a child, a big person must let a child's current emotional state—often hinted at through the needs barometer but also impacted by that child's broader experiences in life and in being grown up so far—inform whether this is a time to push, a time to hold, or a time for something in between.

Having used your intuitive heart to gather information about your child, I suggest there are then 3 general ways to respond. These 3 "zones" of responsiveness are not discrete from one another but, rather, blend seamlessly from one into the next. It is up to you as a big person to figure out what zone of responsiveness best matches the current needs of your child so that your caring influence comes through loudest and clearest. And once you have intuited this level of response, it will flavor everything about how you understand your child, how you approach the task of structuring her world, and, of course, how you discipline her without damage. The 3 zones are: 1) walk alongside, 2) go low and slow, and 3) do and conquer. Having a clear understanding of these zones will inform what happens next as you work to respond intuitively to your child.

DISCIPLINE WITHOUT DAMAGE REQUIRES INTUITION

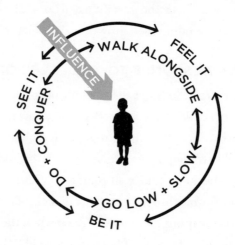

☛ Zone 1: walk alongside

The first zone of responsiveness, which I call "walk alongside," is the place to begin if you sense that your child is really struggling. When the meltdowns are frequent and intense, or she is drowning in anxiety or generally just seems to not be coping, she is showing a very high level of need.

When I think of a parent walking alongside a child, I picture a person who is very attentive; stays physically close by; protects the child from interruption, noise, heat, or questions; scoops the child up into their arms; and gives a lot of verbal and physical reassurance and guidance. When we are in this zone, we sense it is time to lessen our expectations of our child and provide support so he can be regulated. It is a time to focus on using routines, retreating to the "nest," and providing containment and reassurance. Some children will need you to hold them in this zone of responsiveness for a very long time, whereas other children will need this level of respite for only a brief while. You, as the intuitive big person, will be the judge of when you can begin flowing into the next zone.

To further describe the walk alongside zone of responsiveness, let me tell you about a wonderful learning resource teacher who was working with a middle school–aged boy who was remarkably bright but simultaneously challenged by difficulties with his capacity to organize himself and also to communicate adeptly using written language. Children such as this boy are often referred to as "twice exceptional" for their extraordinary intellectual gifts (exceptional!) and for their comparative learning difficulties (exceptional!). Oh the frustration endured by such a child! As the school team met with this boy's parents to discuss how to implement his learning supports and make other accommodations for his needs at school, the learning resource teacher commented that while she was very keen to begin to put many of the discussed recommendations into place, she wanted the team to know that she would do very little implementation right out of the gate. She reported that her sense of this student was that he needed some time to settle in with her, to begin to trust that she would do right by him, and to know that it was all going to begin to feel a lot better. As a result of her sense of him, she had elected to lessen the expectations on this student and just allow him to catch his breath. She intuitively knew that in a more regulated state, with the extraordinary advantage of *relationship* on her side, she would have far better success in eventually implementing some of the learning goals highlighted by the team. In effect, she had capably articulated what it is to "walk alongside" a child.

☛ *Zone 2: go low & slow*

The next zone of responsiveness is appropriate when a child is not drowning in a heightened state of need but still seems somewhat vulnerable to upset, and, when significantly upset or disappointed, can slip back into a period of heightened need. This child may previously have required more nurturing "walk alongside" support—for example, as she moved to a new school or lost a much-loved pet—but has settled into trusting relationships and is beginning to step forward from grieving all of the difficulty in her life to a more confidently regulated state. I call this the "go low and slow" zone.

When I think about a big person going low and slow with a child, I picture someone responding intuitively to support a child in navigating small disappointments while creating a nurturing environment in which these small disappointments can get processed—and larger disappointments just aren't allowed in, or at least get tamed before they can derail the child and lead to a persistently higher level of need. This is a zone of responsiveness in which the big person continues to work to pave the way and smooth the bumps, but where the child is venturing out into the world and is not quite as "needy" as a child in zone 1. This is a child who might need a "mental health day" from school every now and then, or some special quiet connection time (beyond what might be typical) over the weekend, or a "pass" for swim practice on a particular evening—all as dictated by your sense of how she is adjusting, settling, and coping.

☞ Zone 3: do & conquer

The third zone of responsiveness is the place to start when a child appears to be doing relatively well. When meltdowns are rare or fleeting and not intense, or when a child manages most normal day-to-day disappointments or changes in routine with relative ease, she is showing a low level of need that is best met with the "do and conquer" level of responsiveness.

A big person who is supporting a child in this zone allows the child to experience upset and disappointment without as much intervention, as the child's healthy and typical response—frustration—is easily softened into sadness. The big person reassures the child as she naturally settles, picking herself up, dusting herself off, and carrying on with resilience to find a new way through or to accept a reality that she doesn't really like but has come to know as unavoidable. Knowing the child and her needs, hopes, favorite things, and greatest desires allows the big person to offer a nurturing embrace, gentle guidance, and responsive care. The child is able to rest, safe in the knowledge that she can trust in her big person to understand her deeply and to have her best interests constantly in mind. This is a child who is equipped to deal with challenges with less safeguarding than in either of the previous 2 zones.

There are no definite boundaries between 1 zone of responsiveness and the next; rather, they merge into one another. Just as there is no precise way to determine which exact level of need your child is experiencing, there are no absolutely clear signals to direct you to one zone of responsiveness or another. You'll be using your intuition and your deep knowledge of, and connection to, your child.

NURTURE YOUR OWN NEEDS

All big people who are responsible for growing up children must necessarily put the children's needs first. This does not mean that the needs of big people cannot or should not be nurtured and tended to as well—*just never by a child*. There is a time and place and manner in which the needs of big people ought to be tended to, but when children are around it is the needs of the children that must remain supreme. How is this fair? Why must this be so? Children come into this world with no choice but to seek dependence on us. Their very survival hinges on us responding confidently and certainly. And while they might be able to physically survive being grown up by a big person whose own needs took center stage, they most certainly would not thrive emotionally nor become all that they were meant to be. That is, they would be robbed of the chance to grow up in the very best possible way. When children are born, and most importantly when a person chooses to step into the role of "big person" for those children, nature demands that the children's needs be met. And so it is up to us as big people to meet that demand. In chapter 4, I explained the damage that can come about when children become hulked up and big people "dehulkified."

Numerous different personal needs can get in the way of our ability as a big person to respond intuitively and grow up our children in the best possible way. Anxiety and depression are very common, and it is clear that many adults face the sometimes debilitating impact of these and other mental health challenges. Being "stuck," agitated, or irritable, and having a reduced capacity to cope with stress or upset are prevailing symptoms of mood-based disorders, and existing in this kind of mindset can make it very challenging to find our inner Hulk.

Sometimes big people get taken by surprise when their own needs are awakened as they care for their children. When they engage in feeling it for their children, some adults begin to feel the weight of their own childhood experiences. For example, an enduring or intense experience of not having been responded to in caring and compassionate ways by your own big people when you were a child can be triggered by becoming a parent yourself. In other words, the actual act of being a big person to a child triggers this neurological and emotional trauma response that activates the upset connected to the earlier trauma, which may have been repressed and lain dormant for many years. The impact of this trauma may be that as a big person you are incapable of seeing your own child's needs, as it would mean recognizing the incredible losses of your own childhood when your needs went unmet. The task of accepting and healing these old wounds is the responsibility of the big person. Whether it be from a fishing vacation, a yoga class, a house of worship, or a psychiatrist's couch, support is available. Just make sure to seek the support only from other big people. As you have it in you to "be it" for your child, you can "be it" for your inner child too.

Mental health challenges and psychic injuries aside, almost all big people today experience extraordinarily high levels of stress. We are overworked and find ourselves without enough time to nurture relationships and to enjoy leisure time—either alone or with families.[3] If the essential triad to a happy life is enough time for working, loving, and playing,[4] then the sheer number of hours spent constantly on the run leads to an inevitable imbalance among these 3 needs. There is a reason that the practices of mindfulness, yoga, and meditation have seen such an incredible surge in popularity of late. It is because, generally speaking, we are stressed! And yet, to respond to the needs of our children, our intuition must be attuned, our reserves of patience must be great, and our schedules must leave enough time for mental "rest."

Finally, big people were never meant to grow up children alone. In traditional villages, a collective community championed the efforts of big people to do right by children. Built into the culture of such a community were leaders that big people could turn to for support as well as backup big people to pitch in when needed and to care for and nurture the big people who were growing up children. Roles and responsibilities were divided so the needs of all community members were met. And yet, as multigenerational homes and the culture of traditional villages and communities have eroded, many big people—even in urban centers—find themselves relatively alone, with their own needs often going unmet as they take on the extraordinary responsibilities of caring for and nurturing their children.

If your needs as a big person become too significant, the children in your care will know the impact. And when this happens, the natural order of things is completely disrupted as your children begin to feel responsible for taking care of your emotions and for meeting your needs, and as they become aware that you are unable to meet their needs. Any one of these situations leads children to stop seeing their big person— you—as in charge and capable.

Big people *need* to hulk it up and appear capable to children in order for little people to be able to grow up and for the process of healthy child development to unfold. Does this mean there is no compassion for the needs of the big person? Absolutely not. It is simply that the manner in which big peoples' needs are expressed and addressed must honor the needs of dependent children at all costs. Your children did not ask for any of this, and as children they must have no part in fixing it.

As a big person, you must address your needs in ways that ensure you maintain your Hulk status. How do you do this? You might identify and connect with a network of invested caregivers, or in other words, your "village." Creating these villages of family relatives, daycare professionals and childhood educators, professional babysitters, and other parents in your neighborhood is a key component of creating a healthy environment for your children to grow up in. If you become utterly overwhelmed in a moment and have nowhere to turn, you need to find a way to gracefully exit the situation until you can regain your composure. If you cry or shout in front of your child, take responsibility. Say something like, "Oh, it is my job as a mom to cry sometimes. Don't you worry about my tears; I will take care of them." Or, "I had some shouts today. I am sorry that happened, but we are okay." Don't say things like, "You made me sad" or "You hurt my feelings" because these statements just push responsibility for your adult emotions onto your child. Find other big people with whom to share and on whom to depend: a friend, a partner, a counselor. Remember, it is not that big people cannot have needs or should not have those needs taken care of; rather, it's that a child must never be the one taking care of them.

☛ Dealing with situations when big people do not agree

What do you do when you and your spouse do not agree? Or you and your child's teacher? Maybe your partner is determined to exact some "tough love" but you know this will completely overwhelm your children. Maybe your child's teacher seems unable or unwilling to really feel the needs of your child. Regardless of the situation, addressing it thoughtfully and with a full awareness of the impact on your child is key. It is not the child's job to solve the disagreement. In fact, ideally your child should never even become aware of the disagreement—even though, of course, he will *feel* the differences in approach.

Have you reached an impasse with another big person over caring for your child? Here are 6 possibilities for providing some hope that you can reach a resolution.

1) **PROVIDE AN OUT.** Often when a big person is finding it difficult to respond intuitively to the needs of a child, it is because of a need that is too significant to bear in the moment. Perhaps it was a long stressful day or an upsetting incident has just occurred. Whatever the reason, if the big person is simply having a momentary lapse in compassion and intuition, you might choose to provide an "out." To your spouse you might say, "You know, you haven't been for a run in a few days. Why

don't you go and do that while I hold down the fort?" To your teacher colleague you might offer, "There's a fresh pot of coffee in the teachers' lounge. I'm happy to watch your class for a few minutes while you go and grab a cup." It will probably be obvious to the big person you're offering to support that you are suggesting a break (because she is not handling the situation well). But if the message is delivered with intuition and compassion, that big person will likely also experience your care and will be able to rest into your capable support.

If, however, the big person is experiencing more than just a momentary lapse in compassion and intuition, or if a pattern of responding harshly or without respect for the needs of the child has developed, a more significant, but still supportive, "out" might be needed. The approach here is similar to the "walk alongside" zone of responsiveness to a child but adapted for an adult. Just as we might smooth the child's path by lessening our expectations, we might reduce the amount of time the big person has to be compassionate and nurturing. You might encourage that big person to develop a hobby so he can get out of the house. Or you might make a temporary shift in the schedule or routine that lessens the responsibility that big person has for the child until his reserves have been replenished and his heart awakened to the point that he can come more fully back into action in growing up the child.

2) MATCH-MAKE. In situations where a big person may be having a hard time softening towards and understanding the needs of the child, and the child, in turn, is feeling less than positive about the big person, a powerful approach to supporting that big person in becoming more compassionate and helping the child to feel some more positivity towards the big person is to "match-make." You might say to your child, "Daddy was so proud of you at your ballgame last night. I could see his love for you written all over his face." Or you might share praise: "Ms. Jones told me after school

yesterday that she thought you were the most entertaining student she has had in a very long time. I think she really likes you." In telling your child these stories of positive things the big person has said about them, you are capitalizing on the basic social psychological idea that we tend to like those who like us. You might also tell your child a few things that highlight any similarities between him and the big person, such as, "Ms. Jones was so excited to find out that you love playing chess too! Imagine, you have a teacher who loves chess! How cool is that?!" or "Isn't it funny that you and Mommy both hate broccoli?! You really are two peas in a pod!" This idea is based on the social principle that birds of a feather flock together, or that we tend to seek out companionship with people who are similar to us.

3) **AVOID DIVISION.** As you navigate any disagreements with other big people about what your child needs in terms of intuitive care, take care to avoid divisive comments and actions. Saying to your child: "Daddy doesn't really know what he's doing," or "Ms. Jones should know better than that," or "Mommy needs her head examined," does very little to cultivate your child's sense of safety when in the care of that person. What's worse, these kinds of comments can lead your child to see you and the other big person on a whole different page, forcing your child to choose between the two of you and adding further fuel to the fire. For example, if your child senses that you disapprove of Daddy, and the child is very connected to you, then your child might mechanistically (without conscious awareness) increase behaviors that suggest a lack of respect or a lack of like for Daddy. And even more debilitating, your child might actually feel less safe when with Daddy, adding yet another layer of challenge to righting the situation.

4) **BE BIG.** A big person who is struggling with an ongoing need so signifi-cant that she can no longer see the need of the child, much less feel or be

what the child needs, may need a caring big person to compassionately swoop in. In effect, you become that big person's own big person. Just as you would see it, feel it, and be it for a child, use your knowledge and intuition to respond with care and empathy, and help that big person find a way through her struggle. Figure out the zone of responsiveness within which you are working to support this adult and let it inform how and when you push forward, how and when you care, and how and when you respond. (Chapter 7 will give you some ideas on what being big looks like in practice.)

5) FACE FACTS. There sometimes comes a point when a situation is simply unbearable for a child. You may have exhausted all of the above suggestions and still your child is not being held safely when in a particular big person's care. In the face of an unchanging situation with another big person who is unable to respond to your child in intuitive and compassionate ways, you may be forced to change the situation. Doing this almost always demands that you as a big person find your inner fierceness and, with dignity, compassion, and diplomacy, do whatever you feel is necessary to protect your child. It may be that you elect to move your child to a new school or opt for home-schooling or distributed learning instead. It may be that you change your child's daycare setting, or as one parent in my practice did, quit your job altogether to take charge of creating the world around your child for a while. Regardless of the situation, your action will need to be informed by what you realistically have control over, by your child's perceived level of vulnerability to harm, and by your judgment about the amount of "hope" that exists for another course of action to prove fruitful.

6) SEEK SUPPORT. Parent educators, counselors, psychologists, and other associated professionals often offer support to parents or other big people who are trying to find their way through challenging situations. This

can be a very meaningful way to bring a big person who continues to use punishing responses that harm rather than nurture your child to a place of more compassionate understanding. As you contemplate reaching out to a helping professional, ensure that you seek out someone who uses connection-informed approaches to support children and families.

Regardless of the course of action you choose, it is important to continue to protect your child from damage at the hands of a big person who is struggling. Your judgment about what constitutes "damage" will be unique to the situation, including the level of need of the child and the intensity of the big person's actions. In providing support to the big person who is struggling, you want to avoid simultaneously having the child view you as passively permitting damage to occur. There is no question that such a dynamic is challenging to navigate, but there also is no question that a child *needs* you to navigate it all the same.

Now that you have the See It, Feel It, Be It mantra under your belt and are mindful of how to assess and respond to children's behavior according to their level of need, it is time to get down to the nitty-gritty of exploring what this looks like. Sometimes we are able to pull the lens back to get a wide-angled view of our child's world. From there we can set about gently and intentionally sculpting our child's environment, acting preventatively to create a world that really works for our unique child. But at other times we literally get punched in the face and have to respond immediately, right in the moment, in a way that does not damage. Given the urgency of that latter scenario, we will begin there in chapter 6, with a discussion of how to respond in the crucial moments when children exhibit big behavior. In chapter 7 we will explore what we can do outside those crucial moments to create a world in which all of our children's needs are met and they can grow up in the best possible way.

DISCIPLINE WITHOUT DAMAGE
TAKES MINDFUL RESPONDING

You have had a very busy day. After work, you raced to pick up the kids from school, and you have decided to quickly pop into the grocery store on your way home so you won't have to head out again later. You cross your fingers, unload your littles, and go about the task of grabbing a few things you need for dinner. You can tell you are on borrowed time as you usher everyone towards the checkout. And then Aaron, your 5-year-old, spots the chocolate bars that are exactly at eye level (of course) in the line. He begs. You draw the line. He begs some more. You reinforce the line. He runs out of reserves for coping, and it begins. He starts banging on the grocery cart, grabs the chocolate bar, proclaims loudly and angrily that you are a terrible parent, and declares loudly and angrily why he really needs the chocolate bar. People are staring. The ice cream in your cart is melting. You think about ditching everything and heading for the exit. But you really need those groceries so you have something to put on the table for dinner. You remember that you are supposed to See It, Feel It, and Be It for Aaron, but your brain is scrambled with the mayhem all around you, and you aren't really sure of what your first step should be. What do you do?

The question I am most often asked by parents and other big people is, "What should I do when...?" and they describe a certain behavior that they have observed in a child. With the See It, Feel It, Be It philosophy, it is next to impossible to answer such a question with a single answer because it depends on the child! A useful answer requires a whole lot more contextual understanding of the child, his world, and the specific situation surrounding the behavior. While I can't tell you exactly what to do, I can offer an analogy.

Imagine that you are heading out on a journey with a fabulous destination in mind but you have not even the remotest sense of what your route should be. At best, the start of your journey might seem somewhat daunting. At worst, you may decide to throw in the towel before you have even begun. There are no specific directions. But you know your starting point, you know where you want to go, and you have some general waypoints (the See It, Feel It, Be It philosophy) that you can be mindful of as you set out on your journey. If you apply your knowledge and intuition to the task of responding in the moment to any challenging behavior with a child, you will slowly but surely find your way.

Our need for discipline seems much more acute in moments of mayhem, but our larger efforts should actually be directed to all of the things we are mindful of outside of these moments. Ideas about how to create an overall environment that encourages thoughtfulness are presented in chapter 7. For now, we will focus on getting you through the grocery store checkout line.

GENERAL GUIDELINES OF SAFE DISCIPLINE

There are some overarching guidelines that are constants in discipline. As obvious as they may seem, it's worth being clear about them because when the heat is on, even obvious truths can be forgotten, and children are relying on us to remember. Regardless of the specific way your See It, Feel It, Be It spidey senses have you choosing to respond to your child's needs in a given moment, all of your responses will need to be within the context of 3 key guidelines: 1) physical safety, 2) emotional safety, and 3) intuitive boundaries.

1) PHYSICAL SAFETY. No matter what, big people naturally have the responsibility of ensuring that children are kept physically safe. There is no blurred boundary, for example, around whether or not our children wear their seatbelt while riding in a vehicle. It is essential to their safety. Even if we know that insisting our child wear a seatbelt is not something she will love because she is very intense and very sensitive and will be disregulated for the entire car ride and a long period afterwards. It just is what needs to be because physical safety is a bottom line.

Physical safety also has to do with the extent to which we as big people are able to keep our frustrations in check in a given moment. If, as a big person, you find yourself escalating emotionally to the degree that you are beginning to lose control of your own impulses, and you are concerned that you may begin to lash out physically at your child, it is very important that you exit the situation *after* ensuring you have placed your child in a physically safe environment (such as placing an infant in a crib, a preschooler in her bedroom, etc.). You might take a moment in the bathroom alone or head down the hall for a minute to breathe and regulate yourself.

Whatever you do, remember the considerable emotional and physical damage that big people who have lost control of their own upset can cause by aggressing on children. Research shows that physically aggressive and intrusive handling of children can cause scars—physical and emotional—that last a lifetime and that impact the regulatory circuitry in the brain, amongst other things, in significant ways.[1] Rather than putting yourself and your child in a position of having to undo this kind of damage, take purposeful steps to avoid it in the first place. Children are too vulnerable, too needy, and too dependent on us to have them endure the traumatic upset that comes with physical aggression from big people. If you find that you are losing control of your upset on a regular basis, consider seeking out what you can gently and compassionately do for yourself to feel more regulated as you grow up your child. Information on self-regulation and mindfulness for parents may be helpful, and speaking with a helping professional about your concerns may also provide support and relief.

2) EMOTIONAL SAFETY. The emotional environment within which a child is steeped every day is a key consideration in discipline. The more sorted and soothing the environment around the child, the more regulated the child, the less intense the behaviors, and the more opportunity for healthy growth and development. Think about the general qualities of your child's world. Is your home a place of restful sanctuary? Do matrimonial discord, stressed parents, and chaotic schedules rule the day? Is your classroom a place of safely implemented structure, opportunity, and joy? Or is it a disorganized, unsettling, and/or unkind place to be survived? Even if the environment you have created for the child does not appear to be harsh to your eyes, are there aspects of this that you might be able to improve upon? Do you need a calmer, more organized morning routine? Do you need a screen-free zone after dinner? One of your roles as a big person is to be constantly assessing the details of the settings that really influence the tone of a child's life and world.

Improving the things that might impact the emotional safety and well-being of a child is a key part of creating an environment that is conducive to optimal outcomes.

3) INTUITIVE BOUNDARIES. We've all heard the saying, "Children need boundaries." They do. Children need boundaries to feel settled. The flowery meadow approach of days gone by, in which parents release supposedly innately good children to the wind and hope for the best, does nothing to sculpt the neuroinfrastructure of a child's brain in order to strengthen its capacity for self-regulation. This third guideline of discipline may not seem as obvious as the first two, but it is essential because it has to do with a child's perception of her own safety.

A student of mine likened the child's experience of boundaries to a bridge and its guardrails. Very few among us have had the unfortunate experience of actually needing to test the guardrails on a bridge. And yet, if you were to come upon a bridge only to discover that the guardrails had been removed, most of you would admit to feeling unsettled about crossing that bridge—if you crossed it at all! Those of you who say you would still drive across it would certainly be driving more slowly, in the center lane, and with a heightened level of vigilance. Simply put, the absence of guardrails would have you feeling disregulated. But why? After all, you've never actually needed those guardrails before. The answer is that the guardrails provide you with a sense of containment and safety. And in the same way, boundaries, rules, and expectations provide children with a sense of containment and safety.

However, it is not enough to say that boundaries are good for children. Imposing boundaries in the absence of intuition about a child's needs is not necessarily good for the child and may in fact be damaging. That is, if we use boundaries as a "technique" for controlling children and their behavior, we have slipped out of the See It, Feel It, Be It mentality and back into a rote response. For example, let's say you have registered your child for soccer. Practices are on Tuesdays and Thursdays after school, and games are on Saturday mornings. He is excited to join the team because so many of his friends play soccer too. You believe it is important for your child to have a sense of commitment to the team, and more generally, you want him to have the experience of persevering and attaining a new skill (soccer), even though it is sometimes hard work. Four weeks into the season, you arrive at school to pick your child up and ferry him to his Thursday afternoon soccer practice. All week you have been quietly wondering if he might be coming down with an illness because he has seemed out of sorts—irritable and tired. You also know that the big math test was yesterday and that he was nervous about it. Maybe that is the cause of his irritability? In addition, it is pretty plain to see that your hoped-for love affair between your child and soccer is not to be. He hates it! You have insisted he finish the season as part of his commitment to the team, but it has taken some poking and prodding to get him out the door to practices and games. As you see him come towards you at school pickup, you can tell before he even opens his mouth that he does not want to attend soccer practice. Do you make him go?

If you were to resort to a "technique" approach with the belief that it is important for you to stick to your guns—that is, once you put a boundary in place, you need to hold it at all costs—then, yes, you would make him go. But is that the right decision? Might you need to allow a bit of wiggle room when you set boundaries to accommodate a change in circumstances? He is not actually sick as far as you can tell, but maybe that is coming? How stressed was he about that math test? Does he have enough emotional reserves left to deal with a soccer practice that he does not want to be at? Is it okay to "let him off the hook"? Using the See It, Feel It, Be It philosophy, you might decide that this is a day your child needs to spend at home. He is tired. He is grumpy. He is stressed. He is disregulated. He needs to crawl into the cocoon of your home for the evening and recuperate. And because you are "being it" for your child, and have your swagger on about communicating to him on subtle, core levels that you have his back, you are moved to respond to his needs accordingly.

Let's say you take charge of the situation and don't even let the chatter of "Please can I not go to soccer today!" begin. Instead, as he approaches, you speak first: "Oh, sweet boy. You look absolutely tuckered out. You are not going to be able to go to soccer practice tonight. Come with me. I am going to take you home. It will be into PJs and onto the couch for you. I'll get you all sorted out. Let me take your bag for you. On our way now. Let's go." This is an example of the "gray zone" that needs to exist alongside established boundaries. This is very different from having him launch into the tirade of begging to stay home and you reluctantly submitting in an uncertain way, making him wonder if maybe he should be at that horrible practice after all, and, although he got what he wanted, if maybe his big person let him drift too far towards the edge of the bridge in the process. Intuitive boundaries are not black and white. Rather, intuitive boundaries respond to the levels of need of each unique child in each changing moment. It is essential that we take our child's ever-changing needs into account as we erect the safekeeping guardrails of a boundary.

NINE STEPPING STONES FOR FINDING YOUR WAY IN THE MOMENT

Now that you know the 3 overarching guidelines for discipline that ensure a child's safety, what do you do? As I said, and though it may be frustrating to hear, I can't tell you exactly. There is no one correct path to take. Navigating your way through the intense moments of your child's behaviors can be very challenging, but is also remarkably simple with intuition and the developmental needs of children as our guide.

True to the See It, Feel It, Be It philosophy, you will find yourself quietly landing on some general stepping stones that will guide you along the journey and lead you towards your hoped-for destination. Depending on the zone from which your child requires you to respond (walking alongside, low and slow, or do and conquer) and on her level of need in that very moment, your way through will be different. It may take a longer or shorter amount of time, and may be more or less intense—for her and for you. As you read about the 9 stepping stones, consider that you probably won't come upon them in order. Rather, they are a collection of key ideas that will support you as you find your way through any challenging behavioral moment.

1) RESPOND WITH CONNECTION. So often when a child is acting out, adults are keen to rush in and demand an end to whatever the child is doing. And to be sure, there are certain instances where the need for physical safety will require this kind of approach as your opening line. For example, if my two boys were about to have a full-out physical teardown in our living room, I would, of course, move very quickly to muscle my way between them and prevent physical injury. However, whenever possible, the ideal way to gain entry into, and power over, a situation in which difficult behavior has presented is to have the child feel your connection—that you understand her, you get her, you are picking up what she is putting down.

The reason this works so well is that it is a shortcut to the child at a neurological level, where you can address her needs instantly. In essence, it grants you access to the regulatory core of the child's brain. Recalling that it is through the power of relationship and connection that a child's disregulated brain is soothed and calmed, having as a key stepping stone a response that comes from a place of connection is essential. It may be simply an expression on your face that emotes sympathy for the child. It may be a physical gesture, like a hug, a gentle hand on her arm, or a move to shield her from curious gazes. And very often it will be something you communicate with your voice, using both tone and words. A quiet and compassionate "You look like you are having a really hard time," followed by "I will help you... Come with me... We will get this sorted..." may be just what is needed. Regardless of its form, the connection-informed response will set an important tone for the interaction you are having with the child in the midst of whatever behavior is going down, and it is an absolute requirement if you are to have any success with calming the child in the moment. Connection is also part of the bigger picture of cultivating a sense of trust and connectedness between you and the child over time.

2) STAY LOW. When I was a child, I was very involved in competitive figure skating. The trouble was that I had a terrible time with nerves right before big skating competitions. I loved skating but I was miserable competing. The night before an important performance, I would have an awful sleep. I couldn't eat, so activated was my alarm system. And I was often sick to my stomach in the moments leading up to my skate. I remember how my coach used to walk the halls of the ice rink with me as I prepared to skate my program. She scripted some deep breathing for me. She guided me through a simple plan for how we were going to approach everything. She would give me a tidy list of the 3 things I needed to remember during my skate. And she did all of this with the calmest, kindest, most certain tone of voice imaginable. She was a big person who knew how to stay low. And this is exactly the response required from an adult to help regulate a child's disregulated system.

One of my colleagues can often be heard sharing with her clients that the higher the child has gone with his mad, the calmer the adult needs to be in responding. To find yourself in the mental space of "calm" while a child hurls negative comments or fists or feet in your direction can be challenging. However, if you can really step in and *feel* for him what has prompted the upset in the first place, it becomes a lot easier to find your own sense of empathy. And being calm is not at all the same as being robotic, monotone, or disengaged. In fact, it is exactly the opposite! Imagine that you were very sad and that oceans of tears were pouring from your soul about your sadness. Then imagine that you approached your partner or friend. Knowing that the more upset you were, the calmer they needed to be to have you settle, that person responded dispassionately, "It's okay. You'll be okay. We will get through this." You would probably want to scream at them for this unfeeling response, and you would be anything but settled by it. Our children are the same way. And so, in staying low and calm, it is important that we also stay real. Be intensely caring in the way you highlight the connection; be intensely passionate in how you communicate concern for them; be intensely genuine in your desire to help them through. But do so calmly, with a tone of voice that exudes confidence and control rather than agitation.

Finally, staying low often literally involves physically staying "low." Our brains have a way of automatically responding to non-verbal cuing. For example, if someone in a business meeting is trying to convince us of the merits of a certain idea, the act of physically standing and towering over us might actually affect whether we acquiesce to accept that opinion. And just as we can use physical stance to communicate power, we can use it to communicate calm. Physically bringing yourself down to the child's level, positioning yourself beside your child rather than directly in front of him, and avoiding big hand gestures or movements are all ways you can embody calming support.

3) DROP A FLAG. The moments during which a behavior is actually playing out are not the moments when a child is going to be open to hearing what she has done wrong or how she needs to improve it the next time around. That all comes much later (see stepping stone #9 below). Rather,

try to get in and get out as quickly as possible, with only what the child really needs to be aware of. For example, saying "Gentle hands" or "Kind words" or "That must stop" or "This is not working" are flags you can deliver fast. The reason for speed is that you have to slip this information in behind the chaos of the disregulated brain. Reciting a child's misdeeds breaks the connection that is so crucial to calming her down in the moment, and leads her to feel misunderstood, shamed, blamed, and defensive. A child whose defenses are too alerted will not be able to hear even your flag, much less all of your other chatter. As a rule of thumb, try to keep your flags to 5 words or less. Use a calm and nurturing tone. Get in and get out. And avoid activating unnecessary defenses by saving the teaching about social norms, values, and expectations for when the child is calm.

4) MAINTAIN FIRMNESS WITH KINDNESS. Once we decide that a boundary is necessary, the manner in which we implement it with our children is key. A child needs to continue to feel cared for while the big person is using his "hulk swagger" and confidently holding the line. In effect, what we must communicate to the child is a "no," backed by an "I know you're disappointed" (or another affirmation, such as "I know you're sad, upset, or confused"). In brief, the big person must deliver a "no/I know."

Holding on to the "no/I know" stance is difficult. Usually, if we get going too much with the "no," we quickly slide down the slippery slope of rigidly enforcing the boundary in an unfeeling way. When this happens, the child shuts down, the relationship takes a hit, and further disregulation and acting out often ensue. Alternatively, if we get going too much with the "I know...," we allow the boundary to slip away. When this happens, the child experiences a lack of safety and loses an important opportunity to face disappointment and eventually acceptance in an atmosphere of containment and caring support.

In many of the 2-parent families I have supported over the years, one person is typically the "no" person, doling out firmness, and the other is the "I know" person, doling out kindness. A dynamic between the 2 parents often has them deeply entrenched in these positions. If you are struggling with this dynamic in your relationship, bring some awareness to it. Know which direction you tend to go too far in and try to find yourself walking back to middle ground more often. Overall, holding on to the balance of firmness with kindness is a tall but essential order for all big people. Every big person needs to develop the capacity to be both firm and kind and to hold the appropriate balance when dealing with a child.

5) GIVE NO EXPLANATIONS. When a child is in the middle of a meltdown or otherwise acting out, he is no longer engaging the rational parts of his brain. Instead, he is acting from a place of disregulation deep in the core of his brain. Any attempt to engage with you in a discussion comes from a place of "survival" and is intensely focused on trying to effect change. The child wants to have his way! An emotionally activated child is not thinking about the bigger picture behind why the boundary is important, and more than that, he cannot think about this bigger picture because his rational brain is just not available to him in that moment. Instead, he will try to find an escape route. And adult explanations provide exactly that!

Here's an example that will be familiar to most people. Your child asks for a cookie right before dinner. You say "No," and she counters, "Why?" You might explain, "Because it will spoil your appetite." Does this help your child to accept the no? Of course not. The very next words out of her mouth will be: "I promise I will eat my dinner!" Trying to explain the logic of your thinking to your child has only prolonged the time it will take her to accept your boundary (i.e., no cookie before dinner). To prevent this occurrence, try to avoid engaging in discussions about *why* until it is clear that: a) the boundary has been accepted, b) the child is emotionally settled, and c) you have engaged the child in a moment of connection. In the moment, try responding to the "Why?" with something like, "We will talk about that later. The answer is no."

6) **CHOOSE YOUR MOMENTS.** Earlier in this chapter, we looked at how being able to impose intuitive boundaries guided by your understanding of your child's level of need is really important. Keeping this in mind, there may be times when your child will be better served if, rather than dropping a flag, you just move in to comfort and "give way." For example, let's go back to the example of your child asking for a cookie before dinner. Perhaps, as she asks for the cookie, you are thinking about what a rotten day this has been for her and how she has had 4 big disappointments to deal with between getting home from school and right now. It occurs to you that on this day, in this moment, the cookie before dinner is just not something worthy of energy and attention. Is one cookie on one day before dinner the start of a horrible downward spiral? No! In comparison, is this a moment in which being very firm about no cookie, might be the proverbial straw that broke the camel's back? And is dealing with the potential fallout right for your child today? On this particular evening, in this particular moment, you might choose to comfort your child and then declare with confidence: "I was just about to say let's have a dessert-first kind of night!" Choose your moments wisely. Let what your child needs inform your choices.

7) **EXIT GRACEFULLY IF NEEDED.** Occasionally you will implement a boundary and realize too late that you should not have. Maybe you are too tired to follow through. Maybe you have chosen the wrong moment. Whatever it is, when you realize that you need to get out of the "no" but

you also need to preserve your large-and-in-charge hulk swagger, what do you do? You know that if you just say an angry "Fine, have it your way!" or a submissive "Okay honey, you were right," you will lose your control of the situation in the eyes of your child. The solution is to find a way to gracefully exit the scene.

As an example, let's say that your child has asked to see an extra episode of the television show you always let him watch on Tuesday evenings. You said "no," thinking that sticking with your usual routine was the best thing. But your child has had a hard day and his reaction is very big and very loud. What's more, you have had a hard day and you can feel a big and loud reaction bubbling up in yourself as well. And you realize that you should not have said no to the request because you just do not have the energy to hold the line in a way that puts connection front and center. You know the DVD of this favorite show has several episodes on it and that the next episode will start automatically if you do nothing. You also know that you need a moment to yourself so that you can regroup and take some deep breaths. So mustering your most settled tone, you say something like: "Hold on, honey. I just realized I left the sprinkler on and I have to run outside and turn it off right away. I'll be back in a few minutes and I'll talk with you about all that in a second." Off you go, leaving the DVD to carry on to the next episode.

Does exiting the situation in these ways rob children of the opportunity in those moments to come to terms with a "no"? Sure it does. But the greater risk in that moment was that you and your child were about to suffer an emotional blow that could not be contained, and the fallout from that "no" would be far greater than your child watching an extra episode. So in these moments, exit stage left, pick up, dust off, and rest assured that you will have lots of other chances to hold that line, demonstrate that boundary, and help your child mature through experiencing disappointment and acceptance.

8) KEEP RELATIONSHIP AS THE BOTTOM LINE. What happens when you know you want to follow the See It, Feel It, Be it approach and respond to a child's behavior using intuition, but you find yourself struggling to know what to do? It might be tempting in these moments to fall back on another behavioral technique you have learned or to try to find your words or land on the thread of some kind of an approach. If you ever blank out about how to respond to your child, remember this: hold relationship as your bottom line. Whatever you do, have it be something that flows from your connection with that child.

Think about it like this. When you come home from a hard day at work and bust in through the front door only to be greeted by the reality of what awaits—dinner, homework, cleaning up, folding laundry, etc.—and then you start grumping at your spouse, how do you most need that person to respond? Do you need to be reminded of how rude you are being? Do you need to hear how much your spouse has already accomplished? Do you need to be told to go to your room until you are ready to come out and be nice? There is a pretty good chance that any one of those responses will make you grumpier rather than calming your emotions. What if, instead, your spouse responded with a simple statement of understanding and a gesture of kindness that demonstrated that understanding? What if she said, "Uh oh. It sounds like you have maybe had a tough day. Listen, the laundry can wait, and the kids' homework is already done. Why don't you go and have a nice relaxing bath? I'll take care of dinner. And once the kids are in bed, come sit with me and tell me what's happened. We're okay, hon—I've got you. All good." I bet your reaction would be very different! That response affirms your relationship. It acknowledges your limitations in a soft way and offers some care and safekeeping rather than irritation or anger. So if you ever find yourself stammering and struggling, not knowing exactly what to do, just pause, take a breath, and think about how you would like to be acknowledged in your own moments of frustration. Channel that connection and compassion and do exactly the same for your child.

9) DEBRIEF THE INCIDENT ONCE CALM PREVAILS. When a child's mind is disregulated, he is not able to engage the rational thinking parts of his brain and, as a result, he is in no position to benefit from any kind of teaching about rules, boundaries, expectations, or social norms. Only when his brain has fully calmed will the child actually be able to hear what it is that needs to be taught. So save the teaching for a moment after the behavioral breakdown when it is clear that your child has accepted the boundary and his regulatory system has been calmed through connection with a caring big person. There is no need to be concerned that if you do not respond right in the moment you will have lost your chance to connect a consequence with an action. That's not how it works.

Rather, find a moment when you know the child is feeling safely aligned with you—whether that's a few minutes, 1 hour, 1 day, or 1 week later. This safe alignment can be fostered by finding a way to really connect with your child: maybe you join in on an activity he is doing or you have a warm and connected conversation during a car ride to Grandma's house. It is then that you would want to introduce the idea of whatever incident you need to debrief.

Begin by reminding the child about the situation and providing a brief (emphasis on brief) recap of what happened. Then state simply what you want to be able to count on him to do differently, describing what that looks like, next time around. Secure your child's commitment to this expectation by having him confirm that you can count on him next time around to follow through on what you have described, and then highlight the ultimate resolution and why it was a good and safe one to your mind. The human psyche has a need for resolution.

And often, when we recap a challenging moment for a child, it activates the intensity of feeling that was present when the event initially occurred. In the midst of that emotional activity in the child's brain, it is easy for the resolution to become lost. So call some attention to the ultimate outcome, to its safety, and to the fact that everyone is okay. For example, you might say: "It was a tough afternoon, but nobody got hurt. Ms. Smith was there to help and Daddy knew what to do." And then focus on the enduring nature of your connection to your child to wrap up your debrief. For example, "I'm proud of you, son. We are okay." Or, "You will always be my girl. We are okay." And then, move on. Do not bring up the situation at the dinner table again with your spouse. Do not reflect on the events with a friend while your child is within earshot. Just move on, and have your child really internalize the full end of the incident.

These 9 stepping stones do not all need to occur at the same time nor in the order they are presented here (except for stepping stone #9 which will necessarily always come after the child has calmed). As a big person, you will adeptly leap from one to the next and glance over to yet another as you navigate the moments of behavioral intensity with your child. All of this will be guided by your See It, Feel It, Be It big person self. As you see your child's needs being communicated through behavior, as you are alert to her level of need by continuously assessing her needs barometer, and as you really get your hulk swagger on through the connection you have cultivated with your child, you will just know you can handle these moments—with extraordinary capacity and without doing any damage.

9 STEPPING STONES TO DISCIPLINE WITHOUT DAMAGE *IN THE MOMENT*

STEPPING STONE	DESCRIPTION	
1.	Respond with connection	Have children feel your intention to understand them and do right by them.
2.	Stay low	Respond with calmness and control in an intensely caring way.
3.	Drop a flag	Provide a very quick and simple direction of what needs to happen (aim for 5 words).
4.	Maintain firmness with kindness	Hold your line and have compassion.
5.	Give no explanations	Avoid explaining your position to children.
6.	Choose your moments	Be mindful of your children's zone of need and set boundaries intuitively.
7.	Exit gracefully if needed	Maintain control if you need to abandon the boundary.
8.	Keep relationship as the bottom line	Do nothing that will interfere with the relationship you are cultivating with your children.
9.	Debrief the incident once calm prevails	Start at the beginning and move through to the safety of the ending. Avoid blame or shame.

WHAT TO DO IN ALL OF THE OTHER MOMENTS

When people think about discipline, and certainly in most pop culture parenting advice blogs and television shows, the focus is on what happens right in the moment when your child is having a meltdown in the check-out line at the grocery store and you have to act. The 9 stepping stones of this chapter provide some framework for how to handle those kinds of tricky behavioral moments. I've found, time after time, that by knowing children's specific needs, aiming to connect with them, regulate them, and have them really feel your understanding of them, these moments become workable. It might take you 3 minutes to drop a flag and sort out the disappointment about not being able to have the chocolate bar, fifteen minutes to settle your child into a calmer state of being, and another fifteen to debrief the incident. But if that takes thirty-three minutes, what about the other 1,407 minutes of a child's day? Is discipline without damage only important in the actual moment of behavioral challenge? Or does being intuitively informed about our children and what they need mean we need to broaden our sense of "discipline" to the rest of their sweet little lives?

The reality is that we create and sculpt the world in which our children are growing, all day, every day, and the nature of that world must be considered in any discussion on the topic of discipline. The best thing for any child is to exist in the context of relationship. We want the world and the environment in which our children live, from sun up to sun down and even in their sleepy dreams, to be imbued with the sense that their big people are on it. Within that world, big people play many roles: sometimes we look like the traffic cop, sometimes the nurse, sometimes the bard, or sometimes the magical wizard that makes children's wishes come true. It is through relationship with our children that we can grow them up to be regulated, settled, emotionally healthy children—little people who live every day with the reality of a beautiful, non-negotiable, and certain connection with their big people. And imbuing our children's world with this certainty allows them to become more regulated, settled, and healthy. A large part of discipline, then, is creating that sort of world for them.

In the next chapter we will move from understanding how to *be* it for children in an intense behavioral moment to learning how to *be* it for them during all the other moments of the day. In other words, our disciplinary efforts shift from primarily responding to their behavior to preventing the need for that behavior in the first place. "Being it" means being conscious of how we design our children's world and thinking about what the day in, day out, drip drop of life is like for our kids from their perspective. We want them to be embraced by relationship and all that comes from that—like hope, generosity, safety—so that it is those feelings that are constantly and tangibly at their disposal, and easy to retrieve both mentally and physically. We want to set up our children's world so that connection and all that flows from it is a definable feature of their existence—so that they grow up to be healthy, adaptable human beings and so we can prevent many of the behavioral challenges that we might otherwise see.

DISCIPLINE WITHOUT DAMAGE
TAKES MINDFUL PREVENTION

As an undergraduate student, I did what a lot of students do to get by: I worked a couple of research assistant positions, studied full-time, took out student loans, and lived in the cheapest place I could find. This meant that my "home" in the fourth year of my undergraduate career was a drafty basement suite in an old rundown house shared with my best friend and several large rats. In addition to being drafty (you could actually see through the walls to the yard outside in several spots in our living room), it was damp and, I am quite sure, full of mold. I tried to stay physically active and healthy, but time was scarce. I was up until the wee hours of the morning studying, many nights falling asleep at my desk, only to awake to the sound of my alarm going off. Money was tight, time was tight, and the stakes—in my mind—were high.

Eventually all of this stress caught up to me and I developed the most wretched chest infection imaginable. I would haul myself into the campus medical clinic and get some medication, only to find myself back at that same clinic over and over again, unable to shake the infection. My parents—a few thousand kilometers away—were worried sick, and I was beginning to wonder if I was ever going to get better. The trouble was that *I was treating the symptoms, not the problem.* My real problem was not the infection itself, although certainly it needed some direct treatment, but the environment around me that had caused the illness in the first place. That is, I was reacting moment by moment, as my symptoms and the degree of my distress around them demanded, but the environment around me, and the manner in which I was living out my life, remained unchanged.

When you find yourself continually reacting moment by moment to your child's behaviors, ask yourself whether there is an underlying problem in the child's world that is going unnoticed. Just repeatedly responding to ongoing behavioral challenges in our children has the same central flaw as hammering away at persistent chest infection symptoms with medication—while it may get you through that moment, it does nothing to prevent the next challenging moment, and more than that, does nothing to actually ameliorate the broader context. To heal my chest infection, I needed to do more than respond to my symptoms. I needed to change my environment, my routine, my habits—my world. And the same is true for children. To really get ahead of behavior, we need to not only know how to handle the challenging moments, but we also need to know how to set up a life that resonates with who they are as little human beings, how their brains are growing, and how their spiritual and emotional selves are developing.

LOOK AT THE BIG PICTURE

A child's behavior is born of *need.* In all of my years of practice, I have yet to meet a child who enjoys misbehaving. Rather, I see child after child that is working incredibly hard to communicate a message about an unmet need in increasingly desperate and extreme ways. And I see big people who are so busy working frantically to respond in the moment to the outbursts, tantrums, rudeness, hits, shouts, and kicks that they often overlook the extenuating circumstances that may be contributing to the situation—as well as the ways in which their own influence may be perpetuating that situation. Just as I have yet to meet a child who enjoys misbehaving, I also have yet to meet a parent who has not genuinely intended to do the very best by their children. Remember, it isn't about being perfect; it is about being good enough. And a big part of being good enough is to consider the trickle-down effect of the child's world and our influences on it.

Just as my unhealthy environment and lifestyle made it nearly impossible for me to recover from my chest infection, if children are stressed, if they experience the circumstances of their day-to-day world in overwhelming ways, if they have no opportunity for rest and restoration, or if they consistently question their physical and emotional safety and security, then their behaviors will persist or escalate. Those behaviors represent their outlet for communicating all of these undesirable conditions. Simply put, if the need persists, the behavior will persist. Life for big people then becomes one long-lasting attempt to respond effectively in the moment to challenging behaviors, and the moments come rapidly and constantly and with very little reprieve.

Thus, while it is essential that we respond to the moments of intense need with an appropriate course of action (that only helps and never harms), it is also essential that, when possible, we address the broader context of the environment to prevent these individual challenging moments from becoming *all* of the moments. Just as it is important to know how to respond in the moment, it is important to know how to sculpt, create, nurture, and adapt the world around children to make it the most ideal environment possible for development to flourish. We do this by using our See It, Feel It, Be It philosophy to create a world that meets the unique makeup and needs of each child.

DISCIPLINE WITHOUT DAMAGE RESPONDS TO AND PREVENTS MOMENTS OF CHALLENGING BEHAVIOR

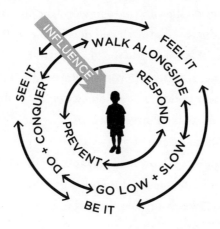

☞ *Mindful prevention: the child's need*

When designing a world for optimal development, remember what we learned about the growing brain in Part I. As children begin to feel safe and settled in the world that surrounds them, and at the same time come to understand subconsciously that their big people are moving quietly and persistently on their behalf to ensure that this happens, their brains are impacted in an essential way. Their regulatory systems settle. And as this occurs, children naturally present in a more settled manner and are more likely to keep their reactions in check when a situation escalates. Slowly but surely, the entire situation can begin to feel calmed. Does it mean you will never have behavioral challenges to navigate? Of course not. But it does mean that with the science of development on your side, you are giving your children the best possible world in which to grow up. You are honoring the science of development by both responding with connection in the moment *and* creating a world that is optimal for your children.

The challenge for children is having absolutely no control over whether or not this optimal world is created for them. Children are like little seeds floating on the wind of their world, hoping that the place they land will be conducive to growth and development. But exactly where they land, and further, precisely the kind of conditions that will define their landing place, are largely beyond their control. It is up to big people to ensure that their children land somewhere favorable. Or, to ensure that their children are sheltered from less favorable conditions and/or that these conditions are ameliorated as best as possible. Children are just blowing in the wind. How it all plays out for the child's development more generally is in the hands of their big people.

In many ways, we determine the health and well-being of children based on the world around them rather than on their specific behaviors. Children's behaviors will sort out eventually—when they reach a particular stage of development, age, temperament, and level of need—but only if the world around them has been adjusted accordingly. There is such freedom in knowing this! We take our cues from the children in our care, but in fact, we are so beautifully in charge of ensuring their well-being. By being intuitively attuned to who our children are, how they roll, and what they need, and then moving in view of that on their behalf to adjust, sculpt, and change their world as required, we have the power to see them through to the mature state we hope for them as adults. All that is needed is for us to fiercely take the reins of control and move.

☛ *Mindful prevention: the big person's heart*

As empowering as it can be to acknowledge our power for changing the world around our children, as big people we can sometimes also come to feel that if we hold the power to make the world around our children a better place, then when things have not been working out for our children it is because we have failed in our job. And as this thought lands, many adults feel the burden of overwhelming guilt begin to take root. Have they done wrong by their child? How could they have let this happen? The danger in this thinking is that it slowly creeps into our interactions with our children. It may show up as creating an overly permissive environment or maybe as losing our hulk swagger as insecurities press down. The reality is that it is only in very rare circumstances that adults *purposely* perpetuate less-than-ideal circumstances for children.

Most big people today are simply overwhelmed, both by their lives and by the crazy amount of conflicting information about the needs of children. Usually, children struggle because they are not getting the level of relational connection that they need and/or they have some significant needs that require an exceptionally heightened level of awareness on the part of the big people caring for them. You will feel guilty. But rather than be overwhelmed by that guilt, hold on to the reality that we all just do the best we can with the information we have available to us. When we can be gentle with ourselves around this, and continue to see ourselves as the ultimate answer to the needs—both known and yet to be known—of our children, we will find a way through.

Challenge yourself to greater levels of understanding about your children's needs, challenge yourself to seek this understanding through the science of child development, and challenge yourself to question how you might strengthen the relationship you have with your children in order to best have them feel your quiet but certain responses. Any small slivers of guilt that you continue to feel are perhaps not a terrible thing. If you must, hold on to those small slivers and use them to motivate you to carry on being the best that you can be, so that your children have the chance to be the best *they* can be.

CREATE THE WORLD YOUR CHILD NEEDS

Doing our work as adults to sculpt the world around our children in a manner that is going to work best for each child can seem overwhelming, particularly if you find yourself in a situation where things have been challenging and it has been difficult to gain any ground or feel any positive momentum. There will be many times when you must mindfully respond to challenging behaviors in the moment, leaping from stepping stone to stepping stone as you confidently lead your children in the regulatory dance that gets them through periods of a high level of need. Maybe it seems like that dance never stops. When you do find yourself outside of those challenging moments and when you can shift your focus to the slightly longer-term work of mindful *prevention,* what do you do then? What exactly do kids need you to change about their world? How exactly might this look? In keeping with the See It, Feel It, Be It philosophy, there is no one-size-fits-all answer to these questions because the kind of world that is required will be determined by the subtleties of each individual child's temperament, personality, intensity, and unique constellation of needs. Fortunately, even though there is no precise astronomical map to help you navigate, there are some tips for stargazing!

As you set out to create an ideal world for your child though mindful prevention, there are 4 key principles you must consider. And while you will need to massage how you apply each principle day by day and moment by moment for different children, you will find some fairly transportable ideas within each one that can easily be adapted. If these principles sound familiar to you, it is because you are paying attention to the spirit behind the See It, Feel It, Be It mantra. In this chapter I will make these 4 principles concrete and useful for you: 1) nurture connection, 2) be big, 3) create containment, and 4) connect to relax.

☛ *Principle 1: nurture connection no matter what*

Relationship grows the foundational core of the brain and governs the regulatory state of the growing child. A solid relationship leads to a more regulated brain, and a more regulated brain leads to a more settled child, which allows for neurological and emotional connections to take root and eventually lead to true maturity. Finding ways in your everyday world to nurture your relationship with your child is essential. Here are some ideas.

COME ALONGSIDE YOUR CHILD TO GET HER ONSIDE. Have you ever been deeply engrossed in a task only to have someone zoom in without warning and ask you to move quickly to something else? Or have you ever worked at a job with a supervisor you really didn't like, and your automatic thought every time she asked you for something was "no way!"? These are examples of why asking anything of someone when you have not first established a connection is not going to work. In the first example, a momentary lapse in relational connection leads you to feel momentarily defensive about complying with what is being asked. In the second example, an enduring relational disconnect leads you not to ever want to please or cooperate with that person.

I clearly remember a momentary disconnect in my own life one Saturday a few years ago. I had settled into a glorious afternoon of "projects." I am that person who loves a day of nesting in my home to organize cupboards, get do-it-yourself projects done, or just putter with one thing or another. Both my husband and I have busy schedules, and having a day like that feels like a luxurious treat to snuggle down into. And so there I was with miles of fabric strewn all about me, intent (and content) on sewing drapes for the living room. I was making great progress, buried though I was in fabric and the general mayhem of being "mid-project," when my husband poked his head in from the garage where he was working on his own project and hollered for my help with something. I would like to pretend that I calmly and cheerfully replied, "Of course, I'll be right there!" But the truth is that I called back, "Work on your own project! I'm buried in mine. Stop interrupting me!" While I need to own my loss of perspective in that particular moment, my husband could have made a subtle tweak in his request that would probably have elicited a decidedly more positive response from me.

If, instead of hollering for me, he had come into the room where I was sewing, surveyed my chaos, and said something like "Wow, it looks like you are up to your eyeballs in fabric. These look really great. It's so awesome you know how to do this and I can't wait to see the finished product," my relationally directed subconscious would have shifted into line with him because he had come alongside me. Then, with me now onside, he could have said, "Do you think you could spare 5 minutes? I need your help with something out in the garage." Even though I would probably still have quietly lamented having to dig myself out from underneath all that fabric and put my own project on hold, I would most certainly have wanted to help—to be onside with him. And I would have pretty happily gone off to see to whatever it was he needed.

The reason we respond better this way is that the relationally attuned brain is meant to resist the advances and influence of people not from within our inner circle. From an evolutionary perspective, this makes good sense. We really should not cave to the influence of people we do not know, who may not have our best interests at heart. The people who do have our best interests at heart, and who will, by virtue of that, be moved to interact with and direct us from a place that is well intentioned, are the people to whom we are connected. In this way, there is a natural defense system built into the relationally attuned brain: it is sensitive to and detects influence being pressed upon it by a disconnected person, even if that disconnect is just a subtle slip of a moment rather than an enduring trait of the overall relationship.

So when you need a child to be onside with you, first take a moment to come alongside him. It might be as simple as commenting on something really obvious, like the shirt he is wearing. Or maybe it will involve noticing something cool about the Lego structure he is building. Or perhaps it is a comment about having reached a new level in the video game he is playing. You want the child's relationally focused brain to experience your comments as "I *see* you." You have taken a moment to notice and understand something for or about him. You have come alongside him and very organically primed his brain to get onside with you. And this substantially increases the likelihood that the child will heed whatever directive you are about to issue or will fall into line with whatever request you are about to communicate.

What if the child is experiencing an enduring disconnect with you or another big person? When a child has a persistent sense that an adult is really not on her side, really does not understand her, and really has not demonstrated that he has her best interests at heart, that natural instinct to resist leadership from someone to whom we are not relationally connected will kick in and take over. In these cases, coming alongside a child momentarily to highlight the relational connection and then issuing a directive probably will not be enough to get her onside. Her natural resistance to the challenged relationship will kick in. In this situation, rather than thinking of coming alongside as a momentary way of connecting, consider instead how you can come alongside in a general way. Keep a keen awareness of *how* you are communicating to the child that you are there, that you get her, that you understand her. And do this without bashing her over the head with it in a canned or obvious way. Instead, it is simply a way of *being* with the child that leaves her with the sense that you are a big person who "gets her."

To repair a relationship or build one, address out loud the things both obvious and subtle that you notice the two of you doing together. You might say, "I see you're getting tired. Here is a glass of water. Let's take stock of what's coming up this afternoon," or "I made a smiley face out of ketchup on your omelet. We always do it that way, don't we?" Narrate the ways that demonstrate the connection you have and let her hear you observe it, day in and day out, over many weeks and months. Do this without pompous parade or presentation, but surely and quietly and confidently.

SHOW LOVE IN A NO-MATTER-WHAT KIND OF WAY. In a wonderful children's book called *No Matter What*, a mother fox, aptly named Large, and her little fox, aptly named Small, find their way to having Small understand without exception that he is the apple of Large's eye.[1] Small is having a grim and grumpy day and puts forward all sorts of ideas about just how awful he is. After Small expresses each idea, Large very firmly and kindly responds, "I'd always love you, no matter what." In this way, Large affirms the enduring belief that there is nothing that could ever get in the way of her connection with her child. Children (and, in fact, human beings of all ages) have a driving desire to know that the connection they have with their most important people will never be severed.

When a child is dropped off at school or daycare, he faces a disconnect from his big person. When a child goes to sleep at night, she faces a disconnect from her big person. When a child and a big person have a falling out, they face a disconnect. Any disconnect, emotional or physical, between a big person and a little person, causes the relationally attuned brain some angst. Physical disconnects are especially challenging for younger children, who are not yet able to hold on to their big people in their mind's eye when their big people are away from them. Physical disconnects can also be very challenging for children of any age who struggle with anxiety and, more generally, with feeling safe in the environment they are in. Emotional disconnects—either due to disagreement or "emotional absence"—will impact every child, regardless of age or circumstance. When you stop to think about it, the reality is that our children face emotional and/or physical disconnects from us several times every day. So what can be done? How do we give them that comforting "no matter what" place to land?

The best way to reduce the impact and angst of a physical disconnect, even for a child who does not appear to be struggling, is to place the focus on the enduring connection rather than on the disconnection. Think about turning the "goodbye" into a "hello." In other words, redirect the mind's eye to a future point of reconnection. So, when you drop off your child at school, rather than saying goodbye or highlighting all the great things he will do while he is away from you, say, "I hope you have a great day. I am looking forward to picking you up after school. Let's use those coupons we got in the mail to go grab an ice cream from that new place." The key as you leave him is to cast his mind forward to your assured reconnection by scripting for him exactly that.

You can turn disconnection into connection in a zillion different ways, so engage your playful, creative mind in being with your child even when you cannot physically be there. One mother I know visited her daughter's school playground in the evening, and as she led her daughter around the mother would leave stashes of magical kisses for her daughter at strategic places—under the slide, beside the swings, behind the play structure. When the girl was on the playground the next day, she would go stand in each of those places, her friends being never the wiser, and collect her mother's kisses. Another parent I know filled up a locket with kisses for her daughter each morning. Yet another family laminated a small photograph of them with their little boy and hung it from a lanyard spritzed with the father's cologne. The child wore it hidden under his shirt at preschool. Tucking special notes in your child's lunch bag is another idea. One mom, whose high school–aged child was embarrassed to find notes from his mom in his lunch but who still really needed little touch points from her during the day, took a bite out of his sandwich every morning when she made his lunch. When her son went to eat his sandwich, he would see that little bite mark and feel her presence.

To turn disconnection into connection at bedtime, I have seen parents script for children a connection they will have in their dreams that night. Or after their child falls asleep, leave in their child's bed a special stuffy as proof of their visit to the room—their connection and presence. Or sneak a special story, hand selected on that day for that child, under his pillow once he is asleep, with an invitation before bed to find the special story in the morning and bring it to his parents so they can snuggle up and read together. Even as a therapist, when I am ending my ongoing sessions with individual children because they are doing well and no longer need to be coming, I have a ritual of giving them a special rock shaped like a star along with a whole story about how it will always twinkle brightly for them because of what a star I think they are. And anytime they want to be reminded of that or of the time that we have had together, all they need to do is hold that star in their hands and close their eyes, and their twinkly-ness and my belief in them will always be right there.

In the case of emotional disconnects due to conflict between the adult and the child, or due to the emotional absence of the adult, highlighting the ongoing nature of the emotional relationship can spark a reconnect. For example, after a moment of conflict, you might say to your child that it does not matter that you just had this not-awesome moment: "We had some angry words. Sometimes that happens, but it is over now and *we are okay. No matter what, I always love you.*" After scripting the end of this disconnect, you could move to a point of future connectedness that illustrates how you continue to hold on to your child, even in wobbly moments. Perhaps "I'm really looking forward to that walk we had planned at the beach after dinner. Do you think we will find some snails?" or "It will be so great to see the creation you have been working on in your room. Do you think you can show it to me later?" The idea is to communicate that the relationship endures into a point in the future and maintain a continued focus on shared enjoyment, regardless of the momentary lapse in connectedness that you may have experienced.

In letting our children know that there is a 100 percent no-matter-what quality to our relationship, we really do nurture connection. And with connection nurtured, brains simply grow better and behavior is simply easier to manage. Thus, whether it is physical or emotional disconnects, by shifting goodbyes into hellos, by highlighting the enduring connection between us and them, and by creating ways for our children to hold on to us and feel like they can be with us even when we are not physically there, we give our children a greater chance to find themselves regulated and growing just as nature intended.

KEEP RELATIONSHIP AS THE BOTTOM LINE. Often when we as big people are frustrated, flustered, tired, or lacking in confidence, we can slip into a defeatist mindset that has us scrambling in the moment for some technique or solution. For example, your children might be especially slow getting ready one morning. You may find your frustration with the situation is mounting, your angst about being late for a meeting or appointment is building, and you want to holler a harsh word or two to inspire a bit of giddy-up in your children. Whoa! Dig as deep as you can and find a way to slow yourself down, even for just 5 seconds. Then think back to the idea of relationship as the bottom line, one of the 9 stepping stones for responding to acute moments of behavioral intensity.

Having relationship as the bottom line is not just for moments when your children have erupted; it is a key strategy for any dealing with any child at any moment of the day. In fact you will likely come to rely on it most frequently when *you*, rather than your children, are about to erupt.

In these moments, just take a breath and remember that the relationship you are nurturing with your children is everything to them. Do nothing, say nothing, be nothing that would interfere with their belief in you as their go-to big person. If what is about to come out of your mouth is going to make your children question whether or not you are *it* for them, then don't say it. But if the words that come tumbling out of your mouth—words that you made up on the spot, without any expert anywhere ever having officially "blessed" them—are going to put you in the position of really communicating to your children that you have got them and that you adore them and that you are succinctly but lovingly in charge of this situation, then speak up and don't stop!

The freedom that comes with an intuitive approach, and indeed the heart of the See It, Feel It, Be It philosophy, is that there is no specific technique, only a way of being. This way of being communicates to children that they are your bottom line—your love for them is where it is at. So rather than finding yourself scrambling for an answer in those moments, just allow yourself to *be* the answer and find yourself moving in a manner that deepens—and never harms—the relationship. If this still feels like an elusive concept, think of it this way. Think back to the last time you were out of line or you messed up on a project at work or you forgot about an appointment. What did you actually *need* from the people around you in the moment you realized you had messed up? Did you need to be reminded of how irresponsible you were being? Did you need to be scolded for the character flaw this obviously betrayed? Did you need to be punished to prove that you would not get away with this? No. Obviously none of those things would have resulted in a positive ending. If you really think about it, what you needed from the person on the receiving end of your mess-up was *understanding.* You needed that person, in a relational way, to communicate that he understood, that he believed you had good intentions, that he would help you figure out how to get this turned around, and that he was committed to seeing it through and taking care of you. What does all of that amount to? Relationship as the bottom line. And it is the only line that actually matters in the long run. Focus not on the specifics of what that looks like but rather on how it *feels*, and then just *be*. There is no more sure way to finding relationship as your absolute bottom line.

FILL 'EM UP. Everything about how children approach life, what it feels like and looks like, and the energy they direct towards different things—consciously or subconsciously—is informed by whether or not relationship is working for them. Do their big people get it? Are they being grown up in a world full of connection? Is this translating to emotional safety? Are their developmental needs being met? Is this big person–child relationship working or not working? When it is working, children get to rest from seeking it out and can focus on growing, learning, and developing. When it isn't working, that energy will shift back to making the relationship work—with no rest and much less left to direct towards development.

Think about a time when you were "needy" for somebody. Maybe you had a falling out with a friend and she told you that everything was fine. But there was something about her resigned manner, her tone of voice, and her body language that made you wonder if it really was fine. You casually mention something about your upcoming birthday to see if she will act on it. You plant seeds about other preferences, hoping against hope that your friend will know what you desperately need her to do. And sometimes you see shades of connection come through, but other times you are disappointed. You are stung when she forgets to call to see how your job interview went. You feel hurt when she no longer asks about your youngest child who she knows has been sick. And so you try harder. You send flowers. You bake cookies. You call "just because." All in an effort to make it feel like things are back on track with your relationship. And while things kind of limp along with no real conflict or anything, you can just tell that something is not quite right. The problem is that you are invested in this relationship. As a result, until your friend begins to respond with your best interests at heart and takes care of some of this for you, you will constantly redirect energy towards trying to right the relationship.

Children do exactly the same thing. The difference for them is that their relationship with you is not a luxury. It is a necessity. And so the drive and the energy that they will throw at attempting to right a relationship, if they should have the sense that they need to, will be extraordinary. And this drive and energy can become loud and incessant as the child engages in all-consuming behaviors that will leave you baffled. You might ask yourself: if my child really wants a relationship with me, then why is he being so horrible? The truth is, he isn't being horrible at all. His disregulated brain, which is constantly ramping up and desperately trying harder to get everything back on track, is leading to all of the acting-out behaviors. He, of course, will not be aware of the relationship-based mechanisms behind all of his actions; he will just be acting out according to the degree of disregulation in his brain.

Compare the experience of the child's connection-driven brain to an adult who has decided to eat a carbohydrate-free diet. Not so bad, you think, as the first carb-free hour ticks by. But by the time dinner comes around on the first day, you have probably already begun to think about potatoes and bread and pizza and bagels and *anything* with carbs in it. You dream about carbs. You think about just chewing a mouthful and spitting it out. You think about all the ways you might get your need for carbs addressed and you spend much time and energy on this. In fact, there comes a time when the only thing you can think about is carbs, carbs, and carbs. Why? *Because you have not been satiated.* Children need to be satiated in their relationship with us and the care we provide for them. We need to fill them so full of our love for them that they cannot possibly question, ask for, or need more. Only when their cups are overflowing can they rest; only then can they stop driving at having their need met. And they then become free to move on to other things.

Remember the idea of holding on to them so that they don't ever have to worry about whether or not we have them, and leaving them free instead to direct all their energy not to worrying about their connection to us but to natural development? This only happens with satiation. We have to fill 'em up to see them let go and grow. Maybe the way you fill 'em up is by setting your alarm fifteen minutes earlier to create space for that extra bit of morning snuggle time before the crazy of the day settles in. Perhaps it is by setting up special parent-child nights out. Maybe it is by taking time out of your hectic schedule to make sure you are at school dropoff every day. Maybe it is by being in charge of something you know is a real struggle for them so they have the sense that you are taking care of them. Maybe it is by committing to that ten minutes of lying beside them after you have tucked them in, and in the glow of their nightlight talking about whatever is on their mind. Whatever it is, have your children experience you as the endless source of connection for them—fill 'em up and watch them soar.

PICK UP WHAT THEY PUT DOWN. Recently some friends and I were out at a restaurant for dinner. Someone in our party asked the server for some ice water. Although the server had acknowledged the request with a "right away," it was pretty clear within 5 minutes or so that the ice water had been forgotten. And so our meal got interrupted as we began politely trying to catch the server's attention. In a similar way, big people's "job" is to provide for our children's emotional and physical needs. And if we are not doing that job to the level that we must in order for our children to thrive, then their attention is necessarily, and often subconsciously, redirected from the rest of their lives towards trying to figure out why their needs are not being met and how the situation can be remedied.

Our meal at that restaurant would have been a decidedly more relaxing affair had the server been more responsive to our needs. And for our children, life feels much more manageable if they see and feel they are surrounded by big people who move swiftly to meet their needs. This is as simple as following through on something you said you would do. If you told your son you would bring him a glass of water, then do that. If you said to your daughter that you would pack her favorite sandwich for lunch, make sure it happens. If you said you would stay up late with your children to watch a movie on Friday night, be there and watch the movie. And if something comes up that gets in the way, own it. Explain it and make it right, but do not just leave it. Don't have your children wondering consistently whether you are good for your word or not.

Beyond following through on simple things, picking up what your children are putting down might also mean needing to get big and confident and fierce for your children on some larger issues. Maybe they do not have the words to tell you what it is that they need. Maybe they are depending on you to read the symptoms—changes in behavior, facial expressions, a drop in school grades, or a recent inability to fall asleep at night—and make some decisions. That swim coach is no good. Get them out of those lessons. *Be fierce.* That teacher has destroyed their sense of self. Move on this! Get them out of that classroom! *Be decisive.* A playdate with that friend always seems to be followed by 2 or 3 evenings of being unsettled. Stop the playdates, even if your children ask to go on with them! *Be swift.* Of course, every situation requires the careful consideration of an in-the-know big person who can take into account all the requisite details and then make decisions accordingly. The point is, if you see that your children have a need, and if your children are depending on you to follow through on your responsibility of meeting their needs, make it be so. Be the big person who picks up what they put down, who has their back, and who is moved accordingly on their behalf to make things feel like they are taken care of. Actions speak louder than words. Be a big person of action—action informed by the heart.

BE GENEROUS. Nurturing relationship means you are taking special care to see to its health and well-being. And what better way to have children experience you as the kind of big person who takes "special care" than through having them experience you as generous. Being generous is not synonymous with being a pushover. To be generous is not to spoil, molly-coddle, or pander to. Generosity doesn't mean an absence of boundaries. Generosity is that sense that comes with someone having gone above and beyond the call of duty without any glory for having done so. And for children, it is b-l-i-s-s. There's nothing quite like taking a big restful sigh and snuggling down into the haven of your relationship with your nurturing special big person. It means you don't have to demand, seek, pursue, or chase down. It means you just get to trust.

Think about a child who is having a difficult time. He feels uncertain. Life has been a bit challenging. He is intense. School has been rough. He has a new baby brother. You recently got divorced. He is new to your class. Any one of these situations is a tough spot to be in as a child. He is not sure how it is all going to go. He wants his needs met. This child is uncertain of the path to take or of the potential outcomes that might follow. But he gives it a shot. Now imagine that the rule in your house is that at bedtime you read your child 2 chapters from whatever series you are working through and then it's lights out. Before you even start reading one evening, your child—who has had a particularly rough day—says, "Mom, can we please read 3 chapters tonight?" Of course there will be nights when you will have to stay the course, having noticed how tired your child has been or how late the hour is and that sleep really needs to happen ASAP. But what about those nights when you have a little wiggle room? Or what about the night after the particularly rough day when you know that extra bit of snuggly reading time with you is more important than the extra fifteen minutes of shut-eye. What if, on one such night, you were to surprise your child by saying, "No sweetie, tonight is not a 3-chapter night. But it also isn't a 2-chapter night. Today you had a rough go. And sometimes at the end of a rough go, you just have to snuggle in for a 4-chapter night. So, no, you may not have 3 chapters. You will have to be content with 4." And then, with a wink, a smile, and a tousle of the hair on his sweet little head, you reach over to the nightstand, scoop up the book, and begin. Pause for a moment and climb into that child's head. Do you see the thought: "My parent is a pushover"? Or do you see: "Wow! How did Mom know?!" What an amazing gift to extend to a child as you nurture your relationship with him: the idea that you can literally see inside him, understand his needs, and, with a wave of your generous hand, make it be so.

PLAY. There is something to be said for infusing life with a sense of joy and playfulness. If you have been part of team-building exercises in your workplace, you know there is nothing quite like ziplining with your colleagues to launch your work productivity and creativity into a new stratosphere. There is something about sharing playful, joyful experiences with another human being that contributes to a sense of shared unity and common ground. In thinking through what it takes to nurture a relationship, think about the simplicity of finding even fifteen minutes a day to enter into the world of play with your children. A world in which anything goes. A world full of spontaneous laughter. A world in which imagination and silliness reign supreme—and inhibitions, rules, and schedules are forgotten. As the dopamine flows in your happy brain, the connectivity of your relationship also flows. No experts required. Just fun.

In our house, as soon as the rainy season is over, we resurrect our trampoline. I love it when the trampoline is open for business. And not just because it gets our kids outside and active. I mostly love trampoline time because of the free pass it creates for complete silliness. My husband can often be heard on the trampoline with one of our boys, laughing so hard that it becomes "silent laughter"—you know, the kind where tears threaten to flow down your cheeks you are laughing so hard. And our boys, whether or not they find the same humor in the moment as their dad does, will soon succumb to the same can't-breathe-you-are-laughing-so-hard kind of laughter. And with everyone in stitches and collapsing together on the trampoline, it is like relationship magic. Even if it had been an unsettled evening before that, a fifteen-minute stretch of playfulness can change everything.

You can also introduce play when you have stuff to get done, in those moments when you really need your children's cooperation. What if Saturday morning chores were always done to the enthusiastic accompaniment of ABBA? Or what if instead of climbing the stairs to bed, your children got to either hop up the stairs like a bunny rabbit or clomp up them like an elephant? What if putting away the laundry turned into a game of sock basketball, where you tallied up how many pairs of folded-up socks you could successfully shoot into the sock drawer from the door of your children's bedroom? Or what if cleaning up the mountainous pile of Lego pieces became a playful race against the clock? Sometimes it may take a little longer, and sometimes it might be a bit noisier, but introducing play into the necessary if mundane moments of life will bring laughter and joy, and can introduce just enough connection to chase off resistance and disconnection, leaving everyone in a better space.

☞ Principle 2: be big

Children need us to be in charge. Not in a scary, power-hungry way but in kind, subtle, intuitive, and compassionate ways. They need us to channel our inner Hulk in order to feel that somebody capable and trustworthy is at the helm. And yet, we big people can experience so many moments of insecurity when we look around and think "Now what?" And if our children are facing challenges or if we feel like we have not quite been able to get on top of everything our children need, this insecurity can endure. It is especially important during times like these that we find ways to really awaken how "big" we are for our children, for only when they can sense our continued competence can they truly rest in our care. Following are several key ways you might bring your in-charge nature to bear on how you care for a child.

EXIT STAGE LEFT. One of the stepping stones to responding in the moment is the idea of graceful exits, and it can be useful at other junctures in a normal day as well. Finding a way to "exit stage left" without really being noticed is a key component of being able to maintain your in-charge status.

Sometimes you choose the wrong moment to hold a firm line with your children. You might be low on your own reserves that day and realize you simply cannot ride this one out without your own impatience taking center stage. Or you might have a moment of compassionate insight and realize that your children are struggling and low on coping reserves, and think: "Whoops, wrong timing, bad idea. I wasn't really on it for my child just now." What is the best way to handle this situation and still ensure your "bigness" in your children's eyes?

A quiet exit stage left is not the answer all the time, nor should you find yourself having to do it too often. (If you do, it might mean becoming more mindfully aware of your needs and those of the children you are growing up so you have a better sense of what each of you can handle in a given moment or more generally.) But occasionally, when you find yourself a little offside and realize you cannot and/or should not follow through on your planned course of action, extricating everyone from the situation without your children being any the wiser is ideal. It saves face, allows you to remain in charge, and best of all feeds fruitfully into your relationship with your children.

Exiting stage left involves performing what my dad refers to as a "smoke bomb." You make sure that your children are in a safe place and then literally remove yourself from the situation and allow events to unfold as they may. Recently, for example, I had picked up our youngest son, 8-year-old Maxwell, from school and had brought him to my office while I finished up some meetings. I was keen to keep him quietly settled in my office so that the people gathered for the meeting in the room next to us would be unaware of his presence. As I was leaving my office to head into the meeting, I noticed a chocolate bar—kindly gifted to me by a recently graduated intern—sitting on top of my desk. Although he hadn't yet seen it, it occurred to me that when he did, Maxwell would want to eat it. It also occurred to me that eating a chocolate bar before dinner, at the end of a long and tiring day, was probably not a great idea, all things considered. A sugar-and-caffeine rush for a child who is already tapped out and tired?! But I wasn't in the right headspace to deal with the potential fallout from a "no," and if he erupted, there was the possibility of more damage from that than from the caffeine-and-sugar rush. And so what did I do? Nothing. I simply said, "I am going to pop into my meeting now. Let so-and-so know if you need any help with the toys. I'll be just a few minutes." And I left, gracefully exiting stage left. Chocolate bar on desk, in plain sight, ready to be eaten. With this strategy, my nurturing control was left intact, as was my son's need to rely on me to navigate with confidence. But here's a tip: be speedy and adept at your stage left exits so that even while you are bailing, you are still the Hulk, large and in charge.

STEER INTO THE SKID. For children, one of the most comforting qualities in a big person is to appear all-knowing, especially in moments when it actually feels like things are very much out of control. Psychologist

Dr. Gordon Neufeld refers to this idea as "steering into the skid," which makes perfect sense if you have ever successfully navigated slippery winter driving conditions. Instead of panicking and trying to wrench your car out of a skid by yanking the steering wheel in the opposite direction, the whole situation goes a lot more smoothly if you turn into the skid instead. It is as though by accepting the inevitable, the intensity of it is tamed and somehow becomes manageable. Similarly, when a situation with your children has gone out of control and you know you are simply not going to be able to turn it around, think about trying to steer into the skid to maintain some semblance of safe in-charge-ness.

Imagine that you find yourself at the local skating rink watching your older child's figure skating practice. The area is necessarily quiet so that the coaches and students can focus on their lessons. Your younger 5-year-old has asked for a treat from the concession stand and you have said no. He asks again, and you remain firm with your no. And then he starts to cry a bit and plead his case for why it is not fair and why he should have the treat. You continue with no, and things escalate very quickly. He is completely disregulated, has become louder and louder, and is now kicking his feet against the seats in the stands. Bystanders' heads begin to turn, and you feel the pressure to quiet this down and get it over with! If he were just that teeny bit smaller and if those stands weren't so difficult to navigate, you would pick him up and haul him away so as not to disturb everyone else. But you can't. You are stuck, and in fact, so is your child—stuck in the disregulation of the moment. Everything in you wants there to be quiet, aware as you are of the many gazes now firmly focused on you and your child, some of them disapproving. But it will likely be impossible to command quiet at that moment without putting at least a bit of your relationship with your child on the line. What to do?

The answer is that you will steer into the skid that is the meltdown. Try to wholeheartedly accept what is happening and work with it, almost as though you knew it was coming and are prepared to manage it and be in charge of it. You might say to your bleacher-kicking, treat-deprived child, "I knew you might have some kicks about this; it is okay. You let them go, you just get them all out as you need to. I've got you. We're okay, we will get this all sorted out. That's it, you've got it..." What a sense of safety for a child in a moment that would otherwise feel very unsafe. Imagine your child sensing that this is not a scary eruption that is going to find him in the doghouse but rather an anticipated meltdown that you were prepared for all along.

Steering into the skid is not just for behaviorally challenging moments. Sometimes life throws things at us or at our children that cannot be controlled. There is no way around them, no changing them, no being in charge of them. Instead, you have no choice but to will whatever it is that is raining down upon you and your children to be. Almost as though you forecasted the inevitability of the situation, and more than that, are confident you can figure it out. It's like saying, "Just take my hand, little child of mine, and I will lead you through this difficult circumstance." Steering into the skid is like winter driving with your hulk swagger on.

BE OKAY WITH UPSET. Have you ever looked around and noticed how hard adults work at times to avoid upsetting a child? You've probably heard parents say, "Oh, that's okay, sweetie, we can get a new one. Don't be sad your toy broke," or "Never mind that mean kid; he's just a bully," or "Don't worry about losing the soccer game. You'll win next time." It is almost as though big people are so uncomfortable with upset, and particularly with upset experienced by children, that we contort ourselves in all sorts of ways to minimize or eliminate that feeling for our children. There are certainly times when a child's level of need requires that you soften and smooth the way. But when children are moving along and doing reasonably well, not only is the opportunity to experience upset okay, it is actually essential for growth.

If your children never have the opportunity to feel mad or sad or any emotion other than "happy and okay," how will their brains and hearts ever sort out how to manage them? Recall that the basic principle of neurological development and brain growth is that "neurons that fire together, wire together."[2] Life is going to rain down on your children at one point or another, and part of healthy development is preparing them to manage that as adults. As children, they need to experience small waves of upset, as long as the upset is accompanied by the calming relational presence of a caring adult. When your children experience this kind of upset alongside your soothing, the neurons that are firing and wiring together are those that promote regulation. It is as though the brain becomes well trained in the art of soothing itself. Keep this in mind when you decide whether or not it is not necessary to shush away sad and mad for your children. When tended to in compassionate ways, upset is good for the growing brain.

EXUDE CONFIDENCE. Several years ago I was invited to present a talk in the gymnasium of a local school. I had arrived early to be certain that my tech set-up was all in order, and as everyone filtered in, I moved around the periphery of the gymnasium. My chin was up, my steps were confident, my gaze was assessing but friendly. This has long been the way I prepare for a public presentation, as it helps me get a sense of who I will be talking to and allows me to absorb the energy of the crowd before I get started. As I was doing this, a man approached me and said it looked like I had things "well in hand." He explained that he had once taken a public-speaking course that had taught him to do exactly these things before speaking: keep your head up, gauge your audience, and adjust your form accordingly. Indeed, by the time I was introduced and my talk began, I had already hit my stride. My voice was confident, my feet were solidly underneath me, my passion for the topic was engaged, and my sense of the room fueled the tone and manner with which I relayed what I had to say.

Imagine if instead of confidently assessing and reading the assembling crowd, I had hovered in a corner, shoulders slumped, eyes cast down, not meeting anybody's gaze. Imagine if upon being introduced to the gathered attendees, I had addressed the crowd in a squeaky voice and apologized for being so nervous. Imagine if I had told everybody that I "hoped" I would have something helpful to share with them that evening. I am quite certain there would have been a lot of inward or outward (!) sighs as the audience thought: "Why did I give up a Friday evening for this?!" Why? Because I clearly would not have been exuding confidence. And lack of confidence is the first sign to anyone, child or not, that you are not certain of what you are doing. Especially when the stakes are high—as they are for the children who depend upon us to lead them through life as we are meant to do.

The manner in which you present yourself—your body language, your tone of voice, the way your eyes meet the gaze of another—conveys in subtle but certain ways your internal state. Are you calm, confident, and in charge? Or are you unsettled, uncertain, and running to keep up from behind? This non-verbal "language" of what it is to be big for our children is so important. And while coaching on how to send out non-verbal cues that exude confidence—stand tall, make eye contact, be the initiator, and speak directly—can help, the bottom line is that you really won't be good at it unless you actually are confident. If you are struggling to come across as a strong, assured big person, know 2 very important things. First, your child is probably questioning whether or not you can really be counted on to do your job and do it well. Second, *you* are questioning whether or not you can really be counted on to do your job! Some self-awareness about this is key, so sit with the reality that *you are it* for the children in your care and you have the incredible opportunity to do right by them. Not only that, you are it for them *by design* because nature was certain that you could manage. In the hierarchical ordering of the big person–child relationship, you are the big person. Take strength from that! Check those insecurities at the door, stand tall, and take the lead.

BE THE BIGGEST. As a child, I remember my parents always saying to me, "Don't stoop to their level; be the bigger person!" As the children in your care find their way through the ups and downs of their developmental journey, there will inevitably be moments of upset and hurt. You may say or do something to them that you should not have. They may say or do something to you that they should not have. And you will hurt, and they will hurt. Remember, in these moments, that kindness is arrived at through experience. Compassion is arrived at through experience. Forgiveness is arrived at through experience. And for all of these reasons, when the going gets rough in your relationship with a child, you must be the biggest. You must be the one to take responsibility for what occurred: "That was a rough go this afternoon, wasn't it? I am sorry for that. I had some yells and shouts but they are over now. We are good." You must be the one to fix it: "I was wrong. I should not have done that. It is over. All is well." You must be the one to apologize: "I am so sorry for our troubles this morning. It should not have happened. I love you." With your role as big person comes the responsibility to accept ultimate responsibility for the safekeeping of the relationship and ensure that it happens. Regardless of who initiated things. Regardless of who finished things. Be the bigger person. Rise above all of that. Embody empathy and all the good that you want to gift to your children. By being bigger, you help them experience compassion, kindness, and forgiveness. And when they have repeated experiences of these, they are able to eventually embody these traits and ways of being themselves.

PROVIDE HOPE IN ADVANCE. Have you ever been in an argument in which you can feel the tension rising? You are becoming more heated and the person you are arguing with is getting steadily more agitated too. You are starting to feel that you should hold on, slow things down, be careful because you are coming to a point of no return where one of you will say or do something truly awful. Just on the horizon you can see this point of no return looming. But still the 2 of you continue arguing and becoming increasingly disregulated, and the point of no return draws closer and closer. And then it happens! You do or say that terrible, awful thing. You hear it coming out of your mouth or you feel it flying out of your hand, or whatever the case may be, but you are beyond being able to stop it.

At that point, you may think you are out of the woods. It might seem like the logical time to retreat and regroup. But anybody who has ever passed the point of no return knows with certainty that this is not what happens. Instead, your regulatory core is now completely undone; it has fallen apart and you are utterly unable to cope as a result. And what you thought was your point of no return, the marker post that defined your worst possible behavior, is about to be eclipsed by all sorts of new points of no return. It almost seems that your conscience sees that you have totally blown it, and then, in the hopelessness of knowing you have wrecked things, grants you free rein to just give 'er! The result is a horrible, awful, disastrous palooza of terribleness.

Children already have such an incredibly complex job of holding on to their immature brains during moments of upset and frustration that they do not yet really have the neuroinfrastructure to maintain control and composure in the face of heated emotion. But what if you could erase for them the hopelessness that comes with having passed the point of no return? And if by erasing that, you could reduce the amount of subsequent disregulation and prevent them from pioneering new points of no return? This is the art of providing hope in advance. Whenever you find yourself heading into a situation in which there is a very strong likelihood of your children becoming upset, call it like it is *in advance*. For example, "When I come to pick you up from Kendra's house after your playdate, you are probably going to ask for a sleepover. I just want you to know right now that my answer is going to be a "no." And I also want you to know that you might be really upset about that. You might feel really angry with me. And that is okay. Dads are super good at being able to handle that. So whatever angry needs to come flying out of you with the "no" I will be giving you, it is okay. I can manage it, no problem. We will be good and I will get you through it." And just like that, you have erased the point of no return, saving the child from the continued disregulation that comes with knowing she may have upset you.

☛ Principle 3: create containment

Think about how cozy it is to snuggle down into a great big beanbag chair or to be enveloped in a swaying hammock or to find that just-right corner of your living room sofa to sink back into after a long day. Being wrapped up in warmth, safety, and comfort is, in a word, paradise. This same idea of soothing containment translates into our emotional world as well. Think about the last time life really changed for you: you moved to a new community or a new country, you started a new job, you entered into a new relationship. And, even if those changes were positive, recall that you didn't know exactly how to act, exactly what the expectations were, or exactly how to be in a given situation. Do you remember longing for what was comfortable and *known?* Do you remember wishing someone could just give you a manual for how to do this? Children not only thrive in a world in which they are beautifully and naturally contained, but they also *need* boundaries, rules, expectations, and norms to function. Here are some ideas for creating a safe, predictable, and controlled everyday world for your children.

GET THE SHOUT OUT. Sometimes there can be a build-up of things that are festering, and the rule that always applies is "better out than in!" Children who are having a difficult time, as evidenced by a general increase in frustration, aggression, mouthing off, defiance, tantrums, and other acting-out behaviors, often have too much upset inside of them. Their hurts, disappointments, and other needs have slowly but surely mounted and morphed over time into something disregulating. While 9 times out of ten you are not actually going to know the source of the festering, rather than leaving these unexpressed frustrations and upsets to leak out, your challenge becomes to find safe, contained ways for your child to get their shout out. When the time is right, when the setting is right, and when you sense that both you and your child are in the right headspace to manage without damage to the child's integrity, you orchestrate a cathartic release of pent-up frustration.

A shout-out is when your child's upset has been building (over days, weeks, months, or even years). There are several key considerations to keep in mind as you plan for a shout-out event for your child. First, you must ensure that your child is capable of being moved to a place of *soft sadness*—true sad tears of disappointment, for example, rather than angry, yelly-shouty tears of frustration. If it has been awhile since you last saw soft sadness in your child, put the shout-out on the backburner until you have seen signs of your child's ability to be softly sad. Facilitate this soft sadness by responding to them in the interim in intuitive, connection-informed ways, actualized by many of the ideas presented in chapters 6 and 7.

Second, as you plan a shout-out event for your child, be sure you have enough time at the chosen moment to see it all the way through to the end, even if it takes hours to get there. Know that your own cup is full and that you have reserves of energy, resolve, and inner calm so you can be the big person that your child needs throughout his shout-out. And finally, you will want to preserve your child's integrity and sense of self, so find a space where your child can let go uninterrupted and without an audience. For example, arrange for a parenting partner or member of your parenting "village" to take any siblings off to other adventures.

And when you have thoughtfully tended to all of these things, find a moment to define a certain boundary. Your child may ask to go outside and shoot hoops, but he has not yet completed his Saturday morning chores. Firmly but kindly remind him that nothing else can happen until the 3 chores (etc.) remaining on the list are finished. If your child has been festering, setting this boundary may call forward a very big reaction of frustration. If it does not, either he is not as full of festering emotion as you thought or it was not the ideal time for the release. In that case, simply wait for another opportunity.

As the big vent begins, your challenge is to hold your ground no matter what, but in the most kind and compassionate way. "I know how much you want to get outside," you might begin. "I know how much you love basketball, but nothing else can happen until this is done. It's okay for you to be angry. It's okay for you to shout. You are allowed to be very upset, but nothing else can happen until this is done..." And as all of the shout comes tumbling out, you as the adult continue to receive it compassionately *until it is done.* You will know the end is near when the shouts turn to tears and sadness, and your child's energy shifts from resistance to acceptance. And as the sadness trickles and/or pours out, you will provide the softest place for the child to land by responding with nurturing care: "I know how hard it can be for you. I know you have had a lot going on. I know what a good heart you have, even if sometimes things get a bit tricky. I love you no matter what... Of course, I understand. I am right here. You are okay. We are okay. I've got you." By providing a safe container for the shout to be released into, you see your child move from rigidly opposing your guidance to literally snuggling right into it.

HAND OVER THE ROAD MAP: USING VERBAL OR VISUAL SCRIPTING. Remember the manual you longed for with the last big change in your life? A script is the manual you can give your children to get through a day, an event, a portion of a day, a week, and/or a month. It is like a road map for what is happening now, what will happen next, and what is coming right after that, and it is an easy way to contain the chaos of day-to-day life. A script can be verbal, but typically children—especially disregulated children—internalize more easily if it is verbal and visual. You can buy a prefabricated script from a retailer or simply write out a list and draw little illustrations beside each item. Or use clip art or photos of your children engaged in each activity.

Choosing what and when to script will depend on your child's individual needs. Most children benefit from a general script of their day: "I am doing school dropoff today, but Grandma is on pickup. Remember, you have a science quiz this afternoon. Remember, there is an assembly this morning. After school, Grandpa will take you to your swimming class . . ." A lot of children will be overwhelmed by too long a verbal list like this, so mounting a daily and/or weekly schedule—written or pictorial—somewhere central in your home can be very helpful. If your child's schedule shifts significantly from week to week—for example, if he moves between 2 homes or goes for weekend visits with a noncustodial parent—it might also be helpful to have a monthly script. Seeing the upcoming goodbyes and hellos visually can help prepare your child ahead of time for every such visit. And finally, targeted scripts using lists or pictures can help children successfully navigate especially challenging parts of the day: getting out of the house in the morning, surviving the lull between after school and dinnertime, or getting ready for bedtime. Visual scripts provide schedule containment by mapping it out for children in ways that are tangible and easily held on to.

ESTABLISH RITUALS AND TRADITIONS. Both of my boys had the same Grade 2 teacher, a teacher that you just dream of your child being lucky enough to spend a year with. She has a natural sense of herself as a big person and lives that out safely and compassionately in her classroom each and every day. Amongst the many things she does intuitively as an educator– big person is to implement goodbye rituals with her students. When my younger son was in her class, every day when the children left her class-room she stood at the door and asked them for an "H." It was up to each child to come up with something that started with the letter "H" to use to say goodbye. It could be a handshake, a high five, or a hug. So long as it started with an "H," it was game on. As it went, a lot of the little boys that year chose a handshake. But not just any handshake. These were long, complicated, multiple-part handshakes with fancy up-high, down-low, behind-the-back, under-the-knee kinds of moves. And wouldn't you know it, this teacher knew every single child's own unique handshake! Why do you think she bothered? I think she probably did it because she has that gift for knowing what children need. But really why this was the right thing for her students and why it worked so beautifully was that it addressed their core need for containment.

Rituals and traditions are so grounding because they become famil-iar, often amidst a backdrop of change and chaos. Beyond the big things like how you celebrate birthdays or which special family recipe you always prepare for Thanksgiving dinner, the daily rituals that cultivate containment have 3 key qualities: 1) they help to define time, 2) they have connection at their core, and 3) they nurture a sense of belong-ing. To go back to my sons' Grade 2 teacher, her "H" ritual for goodbye defined the end of the school day for her students, provided a tangible way for them to connect with her on their way out of the classroom and back into the waiting arms of their parents, and let her students know that she must be super into them if she knew each of their special handshakes. You could see the look of longing in the eyes of students emerging from other nearby classrooms that didn't have an "H" ritual. Why the longing? Simply put, rituals create a sense of containment, and containment, as we discussed before, is paradise.

Most families have rituals. In our home, Friday nights are all about connecting with each other at the end of a busy week. We order dinner in and can typically be found crashed out on the couch under a jumble of cozy blankets watching a movie together. Our children look forward to this evening throughout the entire week. On Sunday mornings we cook up a "special breakfast" of foods we don't have time for during the week, and we sit around the kitchen island eating and connecting. In the warmer months, we go for walks after dinner. It is just what we do. When I say goodbye to my youngest son in the mornings, I still routinely stash a cache of magic kisses in the palm of his hand. Whether he uses them or not through the day is not of issue; it is our routine and it's just how we roll. Our afterschool hellos always involve a warm hug. Even if I'm in the middle of talking with someone, I will always wrap my arms around my children as they approach. And at bedtime, I always read to my children. It is how bedtime goes around here. Sure, we have our big traditions too, but the rituals that really breathe a sense of containment and safety into my children's world are these small daily routines. What are the rituals in your family?

FEEL THE RHYTHM OF YOUR SCHEDULE. My husband and I met on the dance floor taking two-step lessons. He had tried out ballroom dancing as an undergraduate student at the prompting of a grade-school friend, and I had, in a former life, been an ice dancer. We found ourselves at the same two-step lesson for very different reasons. He was there to practice his ballroom moves on the wide-open terrain of a real dance floor. I was there on a lark with some university friends. The interesting thing about meeting my husband on the dance floor is that he knew a whole lot more about this kind of dancing than I did. While I may have been more naturally inclined than others because of my ice-dance background, the fact was that his skill outranked mine. However, he had caught my eye and I was keen to impress him so I had to figure out a way to keep up with him. The answer was in the rhythm. The key with dancing is to know your beats. Specific rhythms call for specific foot timing and placement: two-step, cowboy shuffle, waltz, East Coast swing, West Coast swing. I hadn't figured out all of those dances but I knew that if I kept my feet moving with the right timing according to the rhythm of the music, I would be able to find my way through almost any move he threw at me. The containment in this case was the rhythm! There was safety for me in rhythm. And something about that must have worked pretty well, as almost exactly 2 years later we were married (and the instructors from our first dance lesson were the guests of honor at our wedding, where they taught all of our other guests how to two-step).

No matter what life happens to throw at children, having a rhythm can help them to find their footing. I see this play out every year in my clinical work as families trickle back into my office after summer holidays, Christmas break, and/or spring break—all of which involve extended vacations from school and other routines. Families usually report that everybody is out of sorts, that things feel very difficult, that re-implementing routines feels onerous. Why does this happen? Just as with dancing, the answer is in the rhythm. During holidays, sleep routines fly out the window, mealtimes are more loosely defined, one day blends into the next, and life as you knew it has gone *poof!* Like scripting and rituals rolled into one, feeling the rhythm of a regular daily schedule gives children different anchor points to hold on to and feel grounded in. Just as adults are often relieved to return to familiar routines after a holiday, children also yearn for a familiar structure. Knowing that "Monday" means soccer practice and "Thursday" means piano lessons and "morning" means get dressed and eat breakfast and "afterschool" means homework sets your children's expectations. Like an old pair of slippers that you relish stepping into, this rhythm in your child's day-to-day world is equally comforting.

REPEAT SUBTLE FLAGS. Every summer, our family heads off to a major fair that happens in our community. It comes complete with all sorts of yummy food, exhibitors, shows, and midway rides. Amongst those rides is the oldest wooden roller coaster in Canada, which regularly makes the list of top 10 must-experience wooden roller coasters in the world. And I am generally terrified to ride on it. My husband and eldest son adore it! But I am a little less than enthusiastic. The last time I rode that coaster was several years ago now, and I recall checking the safety bar holding us in to ensure that it felt tight. I rechecked that bar probably a dozen times to be certain it was still solidly locked in place before the ride began. That bar was the touch point that allowed me to feel 100 percent confident that I was still securely contained. Each time I pushed on it, it was like a little reminder that I would be kept safe.

Children respond to the structure of gentle behavioral flags in much the same way. Those gentle little go-to lines, like "careful..." as your child recklessly charges up a slide on the playground, or "calm voices..." as your child starts to raise his voice in a heated conversation with a friend, or "remember what we talked about..." as your child begins to push beyond expectations established in an earlier conversation, subtly but surely create containment for children in much the same way as the safety bar on the wooden roller coaster ride. Hearing the flag repeated several times in a short stretch of time can make children feel safe; like having touch points, it is almost as though they are checking to see if the containment still exists. Behavioral flags are not long, drawn-out discussions; they are short, subtle interjections used often to create a feeling of safety.

Remember that children are impulsive by design. As their brains grow and develop, they become increasingly capable of holding on to themselves and exercising self-control. But even then, in moments of excitement or heightened emotion when they become disregulated, impulsivity begins to dominate. Subtle flags are often enough of a touch point to remind children of existing boundaries, cause them to slow down and reconsider their course, and then move forward in a manner that is going to work out a lot better. And different flags are helpful for different children. In our home, for example, we often use the flag "kindness and respect" for our boys. We have had several conversations with them about the expectations for how we treat one another, and typically my husband or I say these words as a subtle reminder to the boys that the "bar" is still in place and that they have just bumped into it. It is never spoken harshly or used to imply a threat; it just reinforces the expectation we have for them.

CREATE A NEST. Not long ago, my mom sent me a picture of the most amazing "nest" she had found on a website. An avid reader from the time she was very little, my mother continues to devour literature and her idea of a perfect afternoon is being curled up by the fire or lounging by the lakeside (depending on the season) with nothing but a good book on her agenda. This "nest" she had come across was made of enormous, gorgeous multi-colored interlocking felted balls that created the ideal place for snuggling down with a book and nesting for an afternoon.

If your heart responds to the image of that nest as mine did, then you will well understand the significance of creating a safe haven for the child who is stumbling along on a difficult road. That figurative nest is a sanctuary that truly allows for restorative rest, the kind of rest that seeps deep into your bones and your psyche and ultimately sends you back out into the world with a fuller "cup." Only big people have the nurturing power to create this place for a child, and it is be especially helpful when your child really seems unable to get her footing. When she takes 2 steps forward and 3 steps back, continually bottoms out, and generally presents as exhausted with life, nesting is most certainly the order of the day.

Each nest will be different, depending on your child's needs and your intuitive understanding about what is required to make the world quiet, to invite some peace into her daily existence, and to cultivate the perfect climate for rest. Generally, nesting involves shortening the child's radius and keeping her very close to home. You might decline invitations to birthday parties, hold off on treks to loud and rambunctious indoor play places, pause extracurricular activities, and delay vacations until a future date. But nesting could also involve more significant actions like removing your child from a traditional bricks-and-mortar school so she can follow a distributed learning approach from home. Whatever form of nest you choose, the idea is to batten down the hatches, stick to essentials, limit all activities, and just cozy up and rest. Therein lies the restorative power of containment that is created by the nest.

☛ Principle 4: connect to relax

Within your autonomic nervous system you have 2 key sub-systems: 1) the rest and digest system (parasympathetic system) and 2) the fight, flight, or freeze system (sympathetic system). Your rest and digest system is more prominently active during times of relative calm, and during these times your body directs blood to the brain and your organs, along with other functional components of the body necessary for life. Your fight, flight, or freeze system springs into action in moments of need, typically when a perceived danger has presented and your mind believes safety and security take precedence over rest and digest. During this state, your body is readied for defense—through fight (take danger on and fight it off), flight (take off, or run away from danger) or freeze (stay still, try not to let danger see you). Now imagine that your body is in fight, flight, or freeze mode but there is no actual danger. Such is the case for a chronically disregulated brain, which is often associated with stress. In addition to addressing the primary sources of the stress and taking action to mitigate them, one of the kindest things you can do for a body in this state is to grant it some reprieve from the physical symptoms that typically accompany stress. These can include muscle tension, headaches, tummy aches, racing heart, rapid breathing, and a mind so busy that it prevents sleep.

Relaxation techniques, including deep breathing, muscle relaxation, and meditation, counteract the body's stress response physiologically. As the body senses the deep, slow breath and relaxing muscles, it is tricked into believing it can calm the fight, flight, or freeze system. Connected relaxation takes these techniques one step further and increases their effectiveness by combining them with the science of relationship. Recall that when children are able to rest into the safe embrace of a connected relationship with a caring adult, their brain is in its most regulated state. That is, during this connection with a big person, it is difficult for the brain to maintain its stress response. Therefore, combining the power of connection with the power of stress reduction techniques has the potential to exponentially calm the mind and body.

DEEP BREATHING. Several years ago when our eldest son, Nathan, was in Grade 2, my husband and I decided—much against our better judgment—to build a house. The process stretched out over a year and created all sorts of stress along the way, but finally the day was approaching when we would get to move into our new house and out of our very cramped temporary rental accommodations. As I arrived to pick Nathan up from school one day around that time, his teacher asked for a quick word with me and indicated that Nathan had been completely unable to focus that afternoon. He had spent the entire duration of a writing activity with his head on his arms, taking great big sighs, trying to think of something to write down. Finally, when she had asked what the trouble was, he shared that his mind was very busy and, in fact, was so full that he could not pick out a single thought to write down. In short, he was stressed.

I collected Nathan and took him home. Later that evening I settled in beside him on his bed where he was busy sorting a card collection, and after joining with him in that activity for a few minutes (connecting), I mentioned what his teacher had shared about his busy mind. That was all it took. In a moment, he was off explaining how he had all these thoughts racing around and how it made it really hard to pick just one out. I nodded sagely and told him kindly and confidently that this must be very overwhelming indeed but that I knew exactly the solution to his problem. He looked up, surprised. Once again, I nodded and said that sometimes this can happen but that it is the job of a mother or a father to protect the child from all of those thoughts and, in fact, I was going to collect up all of his thoughts right then. I would hold on to all of those thoughts so he did not have to be burdened with them. And if he ever needed to revisit any of the thoughts, he could just ask me and I would share them with him so that we could talk about them. He looked at me with a bit of skepticism and suggested that it would be hard to do because there were just so many thoughts. But I reminded him that I have a remarkably good memory and that I thought I would be able to handle it.

He started to share his thoughts—a random hodgepodge of every-day things that were alarming in their sheer number but not actually alarming in and of themselves. And I recited them back to him over and over, without being asked, to show him that I did indeed have them committed to memory. And when he had shared the last of his thoughts and I had recited them all back to him one last time, I told him we were going to do one more thing to help him, just in case he got tempted to take all of his thoughts back. We were going to do some belly breathing. I explained how you put your hands on your belly, and breathing in through your nose while keeping your mouth closed, you count to 4 and watch as the air you are breathing in lands in your belly and makes it grow round. And then, with your hands still on your belly you push that breath out through your mouth while you count to 8 and watch your belly go flat again. I told Nathan that every time he was tempted to try and take his thoughts back, or if his mind ever started to feel busy again, he was to put his hands on his belly and quietly take 5 deep belly breaths. I assured him this would take care of the trouble and encouraged him to give it a try the next day at school. He looked at me as though I had just solved the world's most profound mystery, so great was my power as his mother!

Later that evening I emailed his teacher to fill her in on our solution. The next day Nathan headed to school as usual, and while working through some math problems with a support teacher—not his classroom teacher—he apparently suddenly sat back in his chair, placed his hands on his belly, and began to breathe deeply and rhythmically as we had practiced the night before. You can imagine the support teacher's surprise! She was a little concerned and asked him if he was all right, and Nathan assured her that he was just chasing away his busy mind with some belly breaths. Of course, the support teacher quickly communicated all of this to the classroom teacher who confirmed that, indeed, this was our approach to sorting things out for Nathan.

That afternoon when I arrived to pick Nathan up, I was a couple of minutes early and stood in the hallway outside of his classroom, looking in. There he was, sitting in the sharing chair at the front of the class with all of his classmates sitting crisscross applesauce on the floor in front of him. He was confidently asking if any of them ever had very busy minds—to which they all raised enthusiastic hands confirming that such was the case. He then told them, with an air of surprise and utter certainty, that it was not their job to hold on to their thoughts. In fact, it was their parents' job, and that if busy-mind thoughts were a problem for them, they should all go straight home and give these thoughts to their parents. And further, should they ever be tempted to let their busy-mind thoughts back in, they could just take 5 belly breaths to chase away the thoughts. And then he went on to explain exactly how to do a belly breath. Problem. Solved.

So what exactly went on here? Was it the busy-thoughts intervention or the deep breathing that really helped Nathan to find a calmer state? It was actually both. I came up with the busy-thoughts intervention on the spot so he would feel as though the entire situation was very much under control. It wasn't some evidence-based phenom of an intervention! Just a mom being in charge. And because I was bringing it under control, he was able to rest into that idea with confidence, such was the depth of our relationship. I introduced the deep breathing to physiologically counteract the ramping up of his stressed mind. But because *I* introduced the deep breathing, he connected any mention or practice of it with me, which gave him the best of both worlds: a physiological counterpoint to stress *and* the benefit of relational connection with me as it all went down. And that is what is meant by connected relaxation. For deep breathing specifically, find ways to introduce this technique that are age appropriate *and* that have your child practice deep breathing while you are snuggling her or otherwise physically close to her, or have her visualize you as she practices the deep breathing you have learned together. It is in these moments that the amazing synergy of deep breathing and connection calm and regulate your child, reducing her stress.

Belly breathing is one of many deep breathing scripts and ideas that exist. Try getting your child to imagine a birthday cake with the same number of candles as his age. Then ask him to hold up that number of fingers and, taking deep breaths, blow down those "candles" one by one. Or have him blow bubbles to encourage big breaths. Or if he is old enough, he could blow up a balloon to get the deep breaths flowing. There are so many possibilities! The bottom line is that the combination of these ideas *with* connection to you or another big person makes the child's world go 'round; it is this connected part that allows the breath to magically reduce your child's stress.

RELAXATION/MEDITATION SCRIPTS. A wonderful friend recently texted me to arrange a Saturday evening get-together for our families for no other reason than to find the "joy" in that day. I thought it was a perfectly lovely idea! Only once they had arrived and we were well into an evening of enjoying one another's company did she reveal the need behind the evening. It had been a very difficult week with work and life, and she had been yearning for an escape from the things weighing down on her mind. In finding herself and her family solidly embraced in the warmth of friendship and fun, her mind became full of the kinds of things that feel good. Our laughter chased away the negative, and the calmness of our time together was the perfect antidote for her stress. This is exactly how relaxation and meditation scripts work in connection with those you love.

These scripts are meant to take the mind's focus away from ongoing stress and redirect it to ideas and thoughts that encourage calm. As the mind's focus is redirected, the brain and the body are also redirected away from fight, flight, or freeze responses to rest and digest. And more than that, the ideas you plant with the script can actually take root, "stick," and provide you with a more positive jumping-off point after your meditation/relaxation activity is through. Once again, just as with deep breathing, the power of this technique—especially for children—grows when a big person is involved.

For example, one of our children loved listening to meditations at bed-time. We would snuggle together, and he would lose himself in the tale of what it must be like to be a snowflake floating on the wind, or how it must feel to dive underwater and find treasure. He was usually sound asleep by the time the ten-minute script was complete. In contrast, a friend of mine sings worship songs with her child, who likes to focus on the meaning of the words and, I am sure, on the comforting sound of her mother's voice. Both of our children have adored being read to in the evenings, and I am convinced it is the lulling rhythm of our familiar voices alongside the escapist adventures in the stories being read that holds such appeal for them. It is a way to connect while the mind redirects from the stresses of the day to thoughts of something lovely. And with the mind redirected, the brain settles, the body calms, and sleep and restorative mental rest are more readily available. Of course, with a calm, restored mind comes a more regulated brain and, with that, a more settled child.

PROGRESSIVE MUSCLE RELAXATION. I vividly remember the first time I experienced progressive muscle relaxation. And more than the actual process, I remember how remarkably wonderful my physical self felt at the end. It was quite literally a release for all of the muscles in my body that had previously been tensed. Progressive muscle relaxation, which is often combined with deep breathing to fully relax the body, usually involves somebody walking you through a script that moves through the large muscles of your extremities on up to the tiny muscles of your face, giving you instructions on how to tense and release each one. What I recall from that first time was the soothing sound of my friend's voice as she read the words to me and that her close presence—just as much as tensing and releasing my muscles—provided that relief.

And so it is for children as well. A child being lead through a progres-sive muscle relaxation script read by one of her special big people is likely to experience wonderful relief. Even a child who is not actively stressed will know the connection and relaxation that comes with this type of an activity. Some parents record themselves delivering the relaxation script so that their child can "connect" even if the parent has to travel for work. The more you can build in connection—through voice, proximity, snuggling, etc.—the more likely the progressive muscle relaxation will lead to your child finding calm, even in her otherwise hectic world.

CALMING BOARDS. Just as scripting is really helpful for providing containment to children in their day-to-day world, it can also help to facilitate connected relaxation. The challenge for many children is that the moments during which some connected relaxation would be most helpful are also typically the moments in which they are escalating into an increasingly disregulated state. And a disregulated brain does not usually sit back logically and walk itself through a sequential relaxation activity like deep breathing. That's when a script can help. Typically, a calming board involves 5 to 6 steps that are illustrated using clip art or actual pictures of you and your child engaged in your chosen relaxation activity together. Keep the script simple so your child does not have too much to think through in the moment, and consider making it pocket sized so your child can tuck it into the pocket of his pants or backpack and carry it around with him. Laminate the script for durability, and sprinkle it with your magic calming dust or deposit into it a flow of kisses for even more "connectedness." When your child turns to rely on it, you are there, guiding him through, even if you are not physically there.

SELF-CARE

We have discussed a lot of different examples and ideas about how to sculpt the world around your children so they can grow and develop in the most optimal way. But we have not yet addressed one essential component of "the world around the child," and that is YOU. What if you are stressed? What if you are slammed busy? What if, in your world, what you need is lacking? You cannot properly *be* it for your children until you take care of yourself. Consider the following analogy. Before any passenger airplane takes off, the flight attendants demonstrate how to use the oxygen masks that will drop from the ceiling in the unlikely event of cabin depressurization. They always tell you to ensure your own mask is securely in place and working before helping your children with their masks. Why? Because you are of absolutely no use to anybody if you are lying on the ground gasping for air or passed out! The same is true every day: to live out your responsibilities to the children you are growing up, you must be in your best possible form. So do your due diligence in taking care of your own health and well-being.

Take a hard and honest look at your schedule. How available are you to your children? Is there anything you could shift, give up, change around to make yourself more available—physically and/or emotionally—to meet the needs of your children? Also consider your mental health. Are you battling anxiety or depression? Have you sought support for yourself? Do you have someone you could turn to? Even if you are not experiencing a persistent mental health issue, how do you deal with the upsets of normal adult life—a bad day at work, a disagreement with a friend? How do you protect your child from these upsets? Are you properly able to manage any tension and instability in your marriage? Do you have outlets? Do you have support? Beyond your mental and emotional health, is your physical health a concern? Are you active enough that you have the energy and stamina needed to be a big person to a child 24/7? Do you have support?

While we need to take care of ourselves so that we can be the best possible big people for our children, we also need to embrace the idea that we were never meant to go this alone. We know that historically the different members of a village, all clear on their roles and responsibilities, would catch big people when we fell, would step in for us when we could not look after our children ourselves, and would provide wisdom to us as we worked to be our best big selves. In a 2010 documentary film called *Babies,* director Thomas Balmès follows 4 babies in 4 different countries from birth to their first birthday. One of the babies is a little boy from a rural area in Namibia in southern Africa, and it is remarkable to watch the community that surrounds this little boy and his mother. She is surely not going it alone! And the child, in turn, feels the support of an entire community—sometimes directly and sometimes through the support offered to his mother so that she might better care for him. This is the kind of world that children and big people are meant to be living in. Our brains were quite literally designed for such a world, a world decidedly more relational in flavor.[3]

Recently I listened to a radio program about the fastest growing prejudice in Canada: ageism. The researchers being interviewed indicated that young people in North America are becoming afraid of, and even ostracizing, older generations simply because they are no longer accustomed to being around them. Although there are some exceptions, in Canada we generally do not live with our extended families and we have little access to our elders to guide us or step in as "surrogate" big people when we are tired or otherwise needy. In the absence of a naturally existing relational world full of support for big people and the children we are growing up, we are left to seek out our "villages" and backfill this void.

You might focus on forging friendships with the parents and families of all of your children's friends. You might find a village nested within your world, perhaps through your religious community or your children's school community. Maybe you have a group of friends that bond together and find ways to support one another. Or maybe you literally relocate to live closer to your extended family for support. As you work to care for yourself and your children, you will need the support of a village—so seek out that village! Find a way to grow it and nurture it in and of itself. For as the proverb goes, it does indeed take a village to raise a child, and an essential feature of your child's optimal world should be as many caring big people as you can find.

SEE IT, FEEL IT, AND, MOST OF ALL, BE IT

Think about mindful prevention this way. There are moments that will require targeted action: moments when your children are deeply frustrated and challenging behaviors pour out of them. And then there are all the other moments: moments that define life and, for most children, that give it a hue or a flavor. Just as a lingering chest infection cannot be cured in a damp, moldy, sleep-deprived, stressed-out world, children's behavioral challenges cannot really be addressed without taking a wide-angled view of their life and wondering how you might set that world up to champion development and foster regulation. When we know our children, when we have a deep and profound connection to them, when we understand our children's needs and then apply this knowledge to their whole world, we can sculpt the best possible world for them. When you think about your children and how to grow them up in the best possible way, what is the hue or flavor that you think would be ideal? Dare yourself to dream about the ideal. Dare yourself to feel what comes with this ideal for your children, and for yourself. Now *be it*. Go and flavor all of those "other" moments with the kind of drip-drop-drip-drop that will fill them up with something fantastically wonderful. See the need, feel it deep in your soul, and be inspired to . . . *be*.

MINDFUL SUPPORT FOR
EXCEPTIONAL KIDS

How many times have you heard the following: "Cut from the same cloth but so different!" or "Why can he manage one day but then totally fall apart the next?" or "I do not understand how something so small can be such a big deal?" These kinds of comments often fall from the mouths of big people growing up children who are exceptional. By exceptional, I mean children with a heightened level of need in one area or another. These children may at first seem to totally fly in the face of logic and reason; however, when their needs and experiences are deeply understood, it is clear that the behaviors and the different ways they present exist for good reason.

Although the situations, stories, and symptoms of exceptional children vary, the source of their heightened need is common to all: a nervous system primed for reactivity *and* a core belief system about self and the safety of the environment they live in that perpetuates the experiences absorbed by the nervous system. Which came first—the sensitive nervous system or the experiences that primed the core beliefs—changes from child to child, and in some children sensitivity and experience present at the same time and interact with each other to create exceptionality. Regardless of its origin, what you need to know about exceptionality is that it makes growing up challenging at times—for the child and for you. However, when big people understand the needs of exceptional children, we are much better positioned to actually *feel* alongside them, and in response, *be* what they need us to be.

Why are some children more "sensitive" than others? First, genetics and birth experiences do seem to play a role. In the grand continuum of temperament and personality, some children are just born with a hypersensitive nervous system that experiences life with a lot of intensity. It appears that such sensitivity can also be brought on and/or exacerbated by a traumatic birth experience. Children who are born after a very long or precipitous labor, children who are in distress during labor, and children who are briefly deprived of oxygen upon delivery appear to have more sensitive nervous systems. Scientists believe that the emergence of sensitivity as a result of the birth process is related to the impact of the birth experience on the formation of key neurological networks in the brain.

Whether by genetics, birth experience, or both, the resulting sensitivity can be to sound (loud noises, loud public restroom toilets, etc.), taste, touch (tags in clothes, seams in socks, wet diapers, sticky hands), light (sunlight, screen exposure), and so on. It can also present as emotional sensitivity, in which children have magnified responses (for example, disapproval that is internalized in catastrophic proportions, disappointment that rattles a child to the core, happiness that puts the child off-kilter). Exceptional children can display sensitivity in only one of these areas or in a complicated combination that involves several different areas.

Pearl S. Buck, author and humanitarian, summed up the lived experience of the sensitive person beautifully: "A touch is a blow, a sound is a noise, a misfortune is a tragedy, a joy is an ecstasy, a friend is a lover, a lover is a god, and failure is death."[1] The intensity of the sensitive child's existence can really be felt in Buck's words. Indeed, these children may develop beliefs about the world that leave them to understand it as abrasive and generally unsafe. And in this state of heightened sensitivity, children find themselves more frequently disregulated, and much more in need of the safety and regulation brought by connection with a special big person.

In addition to genetics and birth experience, exceptional circumstances can lead to exceptionality. Certain fundamental experiences in life can actually impact neurological development and sculpt core belief systems. These experiences can include, but are not limited to, 1) frustrations arising from a learning difference that causes children to expend much effort and energy just getting through a typical day, 2) frustrations arising from a developmental challenge that causes children to face ongoing disapproval, 3) wounding arising from changes in primary caregivers (through adoption, placement in foster care, and sometimes with divorce and blended families—especially if divisive and traumatic) that cause children to perpetually seek connection, and 4) damage arising from the impact of maltreatment, neglect, or trauma that cause children to shut down or fear connection. Given that children's need for connection with their special big people is essential to their survival, any significant threat to, or disruption of, this connection is experienced catastrophically and traumatically.

While it may seem obvious that children can experience divorce, maltreatment, or neglect as a rupture in the connection with their big people, what is often overlooked is that children can experience this same rupture in the connection with their big people on a day-to-day basis even when the big people have nothing to do with the trauma or challenges. The reason is that it is big people's foundational role to protect children. So whether it is fair or not, children subconsciously interpret the experience of a difficult time in their life or a traumatic event as a lapse in connection with the big people who are supposed to protect them. Quite simply, the special big people were not there to keep them safe, to smooth the way, and to make it be okay.

In the face of any catastrophic threat or disruption to children's connection with their big person, something very significant happens in the brain. The brain of the developing child is unlike the adult brain. An adult brain responds to a traumatic or highly unsettling experience by incorporating it into an already existing "scaffold of memories" that has accumulated during a person's life. A child's brain does not have the same accumulation of memories to buffer the traumatic experience and it is therefore much more susceptible to the neurological impact of the experience. In some children, the experience of the traumatic event becomes the primary organizing experience of the brain,[2] and a brain that is being organized primarily by trauma and disconnection is a brain that will be very challenged to regulate and settle. Rather, it is necessarily primed to be vigilant, sensitive, and alert to any future impending threat. And it is expending so much energy on this task that it is not able to carry out all of the other requests that are being made of it. This is a brain that may be challenged to sit and focus in math class. This is a brain that may have a difficult time hanging on to the details of an instruction just delivered to it. This is a brain that may react strongly and quickly to only a small slight. And most importantly, this is a brain that needs to be carefully held and fiercely protected, with its healthy development championed above any need, barrier, or demand the world may press upon it. These are the brains of exceptional children.

Even in the case of less catastrophic threats, and more generally speaking, *any* child presenting with a need that has gone unmet will experience a wave of disconnection from her big people. Internally her brain is asking: How can they not understand me? How can they not know me? How can they not see a way through for me? Subconsciously borne out, these unanswered questions obviously leave a child feeling disconnected. So, even if they are being grown up by big people who make connection a priority, because of their genetics or birth history or life experiences, exceptional children are still inevitably going to experience high levels of disconnection in their world. The child predisposed to sensitivity from birth may wonder why he has not been protected from the assaults of the world. The child with a history of trauma may wonder why she was not saved from that event. The child who is experiencing adoption and foster care may have an enduring mistrust of the big person–child relationship. The child with learning differences or developmental exceptionalities may subconsciously question why her big people have not sorted out how to give her what she needs. In other words, the uniting feature of all pathways to exceptionality is children's connectedness with their big people having been challenged or called into question. Again, *this is not always because of big people who were not doing their jobs but rather because the job required of the big people is extraordinarily exceptional in its complexity and magnitude. Especially for exceptional children, adults must always remember that the success of our efforts is not determined by how well the child is behaving. Rather, the success of our efforts is judged by how well we are behaving.*

If we can consistently *be* for a child what it is that she needs, and if we can hold to this over the longer term, then the child will grow and develop. And that, right there, is the magic one-two punch: combine optimal experiences with the natural progression of development and children will flourish. The results may not be visible immediately, and this could not be more true than for the exceptional child, but the results will be visible eventually. The focus must always be on the greater purpose of growing up the child in the best possible way rather than on finding him behaving well right now. The goal is optimal development, not good behavior, for with optimal development, good behavior will come. But good behavior will forever be elusive with stunted development.

In my experience as a psychologist, the reason that families with exceptional children are referred to me is often related to the damage done to the child by traditional disciplinary methods. The disruptive behaviors that have become problematic and exhausting to the big people–child dynamic are not born of the child's sensitive system alone, but of the additional difficulties brought about because of how they are being responded to.

If a sensitive child blows up over a relatively minor disappointment and is then reacted to in a harsh way, he is given yet another thing to be disregulated about—that is, his big person's upset—which will lead to yet more behaviors. This is the discipline vortex in action for big people growing up an exceptional child. This vulnerability to a feedback loop of persistent disregulation is very real for any exceptional child. And it makes all the more essential the big person's task of delivering mindful responses to challenging behaviors in the moment and setting up the world around that child in a mindfully preventative way.

When you are growing up an exceptional child, you do not get to be an average big person. You must be an exceptional big person who is intuitively attuned to the extraordinary needs of the child, who walks contemplatively along, and who first considers the needs and feelings of the child prior to formulating a response. Exceptional children need you to be big, very big. They need you to be kind, very kind. And they need you to be wise, very wise.

One of the most significant challenges facing big people who are seeking to grow up exceptional children in the best possible way is the reaction of the world around them. Think about the last time you saw a child melting down somewhere in public. And think about the looks and obvious judgment flowing from most of the other adults who happened to witness—at arm's length—this child's upset. Given what current popular parenting culture would have us believe about who children are, what they need, and how that should all play out according to various "methods" and "theories," most of those onlookers probably thought that the parent needed to crack down on the situation, get that child under control, and respond firmly to send the child a message that her behavior was unacceptable. There is a lot of pressure for big people to cave to the naïve logic of this majority.

Now imagine that the same child is melting down at the family dinner table or in the classroom—and the observers are not strangers but actually part of the adult and child's world (extended family members or neighborhood parents, perhaps). The pressure in these cases will be even more intense. For parents who really understand development and really understand the needs of their child, the pressure from the world around to conform to popularized methods of discipline and child-rearing that are not connection-informed is extraordinary, and this is exactly what makes an already challenging situation even more difficult. Indeed, parents of exceptional children often highlight this pressure as one of their primary sources of stress. It ends friendships, fractures relationships with extended family members, causes friction in marriages, and leads to ever-escalating, consistent experiences of isolation.

This pressure and isolation are placed on the shoulders of big people who likely face most days with more fatigue and higher levels of disregulation themselves than other big people do because of the high level of need of their exceptional child. And so, when you notice others staring, hear their perhaps well-intentioned but misplaced comments, or receive their unsolicited advice, the temptation to bow to all the pressure and come down on your child to nip the "bad" behavior in the bud is extraordinary. But it cannot happen.

All children need their big people to swim upstream and, in answering the call to be the best they can be for their children, to respond to all of that pressure with a fierce resolve to *be*. It might mean being ostracized. It might mean conflict. But a child's life depends on it. "You are not managing an inconvenience, you are raising a human being,"[3] sums up nurse and author Kittie Frantz. Your children need you to be there. As big people we are big enough to seek out solace in our broader village and find other ways to cope with our own needs. But your children are depending on you. They have nothing else to turn to. They need a gentle, firm, guiding, kind big person to sense their need and *be* whatever is required. Even when the world looks on and judges you as a too-soft, inept, misinformed mollycoddler, press on in the best interests of the child. If feeling it and being it means you lower the bar, adjust the goals, and shift the parameters for your exceptional child, then so be it. We must do what science and development tell us is right for the growing child. We must stay connection-informed in all things in order to grow them up in the *best possible way*.

WHEN TO SEEK HELP

Parents and other big people often wonder when to seek some extra support from a professional. You do not always want to wait until the bottom has fallen out of things. Indeed, seeking out support in the spirit of community and wanting to deeply understand the needs of children is perhaps the best way to prevent that bottom from falling out!

In my role as a psychologist, I work with parents and children with a very broad range of referral circumstances. I have many parents seek out my support simply because they need affirmation and an extension of their "village." I also work with groups of educators and care providers for whom there is no pressing need but rather a desire to come together and thoughtfully discuss the needs of children. Workshops crafted especially for parents and other big people can also fill this role as well, as can thoughtful and science-based books like this one. Think of these options as preventative approaches to championing the health and well-being of children, positive steps towards adult self-care, and a method to pump up your inner Hulk. Many professionals and community agencies offer workshops and consultation options created especially for this purpose.

Parents or other big people also often seek support because they have concerns about a child's development and well-being. Sometimes the concerns are huge and there is no question that targeted support alongside an informed professional may be very helpful. Other times there is a question about whether support is really necessary. If you find yourself asking that kind of question, think of it this way: is the child's day-to-day life being impacted in a functional manner by the issue in question? That is, are the child's opportunities for development, for his understanding of self, or for his sense of safety in this world being significantly compromised on a daily or almost-daily basis? If the answer is yes, then finding a helping professional to provide some support may be a good idea.

It is my belief, and that of many prominent researchers and practitioners in the early intervention and preventative health fields, that big people have a remarkable capacity to find their way through even the most challenging situations. Again, no one is more of an expert on your child than you are. But sometimes we all need a little support.

☛ *What to expect from a professional*

There are many approaches to service provision in the field of child development consultation and counseling. The one that champions the role of parent (or other central big person) in *being* what is needed for a child is called the "family-centered" approach. Unlike a professional-centered model, in which the professional is seen as the expert who both determines the needs of the child and the requisite interventions, in the family-centered model it is the families' needs and desires that determine all aspects of service delivery and resource provision. The idea behind this model is that it is ultimately the most self-empowering, and when parents or other big people need to step up and *be big* for their children, they need to feel as empowered as possible. In keeping with many of the ideas presented throughout this book, it is my opinion that finding a practitioner who works from a family-centered perspective is key.[4]

In addition to the practitioner's understanding of "who" the parent or big person is, and embracing the family-centered approach to service provision, the See It, Feel It, Be It mantra is driven by a "connection-based" (also known as "attachment-based") understanding of child development. It can be confusing to sort through conflicting ideas presented by professionals from very different theoretical orientations, and so I encourage you to look for somebody who has a firm foundation in connection-based theories and approaches. Having said that, it is for each of us to decide what approach resonates most with our worldview, what is scientifically informed, and most of all, what makes sense for our children. This decision I leave to your wise and capable big person hands to make in the most intuitive and informed way.

The other big question that often arises for people seeking support is who should go to therapy. Should the big person/people or the child work with the psychologist or clinician? There is no certain answer to this question, but consider some key pieces of information as you come to a conclusion. By default, my preference is almost always to work first with parents, often without ever having met the child. I also instruct parents to absolutely not inform their child that they have sought out the support of a professional. There is nothing more derailing in their efforts to be *big* for their child than in making the child believe that he had needs so puzzling that his parents had to work with an "expert" to help them figure it out! In the vast majority of cases, simply by connecting directly with parents and working alongside them to massage the ways in which they understand and respond to their child's presenting behaviors and needs, things settle out beautifully.

In some situations it might be appropriate for a child to be seen by the professional, depending on the child's history and age. If a child has experienced significant trauma, then a two-pronged approach of parent support and child therapy may be advisable. The child therapy for a younger child in this circumstance should be play-based and with a play therapist, or with a therapist who works through play to assist the child in processing complicated emotions and traumatic experiences. The therapeutic process for an older child (typically ten to twelve years or older) who has experienced trauma may also involve some talk therapy. Younger children (less than ten years old) who have not experienced trauma may actually best be served through parent consultation whereby the parents are championed to step into their Hulk role and *be*, but some case-by-case exceptions exist. Older children, especially preteens and teenagers, can sometimes find that working with a therapist helps them to make sense of big feelings and emotions. In this case, it is ideal if parents are also receiving support at the same time. In all of these cases in which children are being seen directly by a therapist, the same advice holds true: if parents are also receiving ongoing support, their children should not be aware of it.

CONCLUSION

A couple of years ago a little blog post I wrote slowly made its way to another continent. It was just a short piece about discipline, but I received hundreds of emails from around the world, some asking to translate the post so that it could be shared more effectively. I thought it was a rather simple post. It went like this:

> It can be seen at any long grocery store line-up. The older brother starts pestering the younger sister who is asking the parent for the 27th time to please buy them that sugar-loaded treat. The parent is becoming increasingly exasperated. The other people in the line-up are starting to stare. And then it happens... the yelly-shouty-grocery-store-parent moment. It often goes something like "ENOUGH!!! I have told you 8 times to keep your hands off your sister. And as for you, the answer is NO!! There will be no treat!!!" One child is then banished to the other side of the cart. One or both start crying. And while

the fighting and whining have stopped, nobody is left feeling very good about any of it.

Discipline is a topic that receives a lot of attention. The popular discipline "methods" today are all focused on making behavior go away so that we can get on with our lives. They are generally quick-fix strategies that have very little grounding in the science of child development. And while these methods may indeed result in stopping the behavior, the question we must ask ourselves is, "at what cost?" What are we willing to put on the line for that moment of peace in the grocery store?

Contemporary science, including neuroimaging and neuro-chemistry, have confirmed beyond any doubt that once children's physical needs have been addressed, the most impor-tant influence on child development is that children feel they can count on their parent to take care of them emotionally. As part of this, the universal fear of all children is that their parent will abandon them—physically or emotionally. What does this tell us about how we should be disciplining our children?

Let's go back to the grocery store and reconsider what our real goal is. Our goal is perhaps not the obvious one of having the children settle down. Rather, our goal is to have our children feel our understanding as we guide them to a place of being settled. Our goal is that their brains will understand there is a way back to being calm. Our goal is that they know to look to us as their answer. Our goal is that they can trust us to keep it together and show them the way through. With all of this in mind, the costs of having our children feel "abandonment," either through our anger at them or through actually sending them away from us to calm down, become all too apparent.

So the next time you find yourself on the verge of a yelly-shouty-grocery-store-parent moment, remember what is important. Be reminded of the impressionable brains and hearts you are helping to grow. Find your way to firm but kind responses that define clear boundaries in an empathetic way. "It looks to me like you are having a hard time keeping your hands to yourself right now. Sometimes that happens but it needs to stop. I can help you with that. Come stand by me and let's see if we can count how many people are in line with us." Or "I know you really want this treat. It is hard when I say no. I know you have some angry feelings about that right now. That's ok. I understand." And yes, the tears may come, the anger may erupt, and it may all feel like so much more work. But when you consider what you have gifted your children in terms of their chance to truly grow up with brains and hearts that function in the best possible way, it becomes extraordinarily manageable.

As I watched the comments roll in on the many sites that posted this excerpt, it confirmed much of what I already knew. Amongst some positive comments, there was a lot of backlash. Things like "Nice parenting—that's sure [insert sarcasm] to grow up a well-behaved adult!" or "Really?!... 'It looks to me like you are having a hard time'... That's how you teach a child a lesson?!" And so it went.

Where along the way did we so lose sight of the child's soul? Where along the way did we forget that children behave the way they do for a reason? How, with contemporary science and all that we know about the importance of connection and relationship in terms of healthy development for children, can we reconcile the use of discipline practices that negate the emotional core of the child?

It is time to change all of this. It is time that we substantially shift how we view children. They are not evil or broken or in need of restructuring. They just need to grow—in the best possible way. It is time that we significantly change how we view our roles as big people. We do not exist to force our role-based power onto our children to reform, fix, and change them. We exist to champion and grow them as nature intended. It is time that the stares of others in line at the grocery store show compassion for the parent and for the child rather than judgment and ignorance. It is time for us to change the conversation around children, big people, and discipline.

What would it be like to live in a society that put the needs of children front and center, and that absolutely championed parents and other big people to do right by children in meeting these needs? Contemporary science has given us so much important information in this regard, and we now have a responsibility to act on it. It is up to us to take this torch of knowledge and use it to deepen the way we understand the children we are responsible for growing up and to support other big people as they do the same. We need our schools to subtly yet certainly honor the child's need for connection in their discipline policies and teaching approaches. We need our childcare centers and preschool classrooms to embrace relationship as the primary vehicle through which children are exposed to everything they will ever need to "learn." We need our soccer coaches and swimming instructors to *connect* with our children in order cultivate their determination and resilience as athletes. And we need the people in our grocery store lineups to "get it": to *see* the behavior, *feel* the child's need, and *be* for that child, or maybe even for that parent, whatever is appropriate in the moment.

The See It, Feel It, Be It mantra is grounded in the certainty of the contemporary science of child development and informed by the experience of countless families doing the best they can to nurture connection while responding to and preventing challenging behavior. And it is our simple yet integral call to action. In knowing better, we all have a responsibility to do better. In being connection-focused in everything about children, we give our children a chance to grow up in the best possible way. And in being connection-focused in how we understand our world, we give parents and other big people the chance to provide this for their children. Let's change the conversation. See it. Feel it. Be it.

ENDNOTES

INTRODUCTION

1   Charlotte Waddell, Kimberley McEwan, et al., "A Public Health Strategy to Improve the Mental Health of Canadian Children," *Canadian Journal of Psychiatry* 50 (2005): 226–33; Charlotte Waddell, Cody A. Shepherd, and Jayne Barker, "Developing a Research-Policy Partnership to Improve Children's Mental Health in British Columbia," in *Contemporary Issues in Mental Health: Concepts, Policy, and Practice*, eds. James A. LeClair and Leslie T. Foster (Victoria, BC: Western Geographical Press, 2007): 183–98; Statistics Canada, Table 051-0001: Population by Sex and Age Group, by Province and Territory, http://www.statcan.gc.ca/tables-tableaux/sum-som/l01/cst01/demo31a-eng.htm (accessed July 27, 2011); and "What Are Anxiety Disorders?" http://www.nimh.nih.gov/health/topics/anxiety-disorders/index.shtml#part4 (accessed July 27, 2011).

2   "The Changing Rate of Major Depression. Cross-National Comparisons. Cross-National Collaborative Group," *Journal of American Medical Association* 268, no. 21 (1992): 3098–105; G.L. Klerman, and M.M. Weissman, "Increasing Rates of Depression," *Journal of the American Medical Association* 261, no. 15 (1989): 2229–235.

3   Bruce D. Perry, "Applying Principles of Neurodevelopment to Clinical Work with Maltreated and Traumatized Children: The Neurosequential Model of Therapeutics," in *Working with Traumatized Youth in Child Welfare*, ed. Nancy Boyd Webb (New York: Guildford Press, 2006): 27–52.

4   Brigid Schulte, *Overwhelmed: How to Work, Love, and Play When No One Has the Time* (New York: Picador, 2014).

5   Maggie Dent, "Stop Stealing Childhood in the Name of Education: A Plea to Ask WHY?" http://
     www.maggiedent.com/sites/default/files/articles/StopStealingChildhoodintheNameofEducation_
     BY_MAGGIE_DENT_1.pdf (accessed July 12, 2015).

6   Jeree Pawl, "Being Held in Another's Mind," in *Concepts for Care: 20 Essays on Infant/Toddler
     Development and Learning*, eds. J. Ronald Lally, Peter L. Mangione, and Deborah Greenwald
     (San Francisco: WestEd, 2006): 1–5.

7   United Nations Convention on the Rights of the Child, http://www.ohchr.org/en/
     professionalinterest/pages/crc.aspx (accessed July 10, 2015).

8   Christine Schwartz, Charlotte Waddell, et al., "Parenting without Physical Punishment,"
     Children's Mental Health Research Quarterly 9, no. 1 (Vancouver: Children's Health Policy
     Centre, Faculty of Health Sciences, Simon Fraser University, 2015): 1–16; Gordon Neufeld
     and Gabor Maté, "Discipline that Does Not Divide," in *Hold On to Your Kids: Why Parents
     Need to Matter More than Peers* (Toronto: Vintage Canada, 2013): 213–34.

CHAPTER 1

1   Walter Mischel and Ebbe B. Ebbesen, "Attention in Delay of Gratification," *Journal of
     Personality and Social Psychology* 16, no. 2 (1970): 329–37; B.J. Casey, Leah H. Somerville, et
     al., "Behavioral and Neural Correlates of Delay of Gratification 40 Years Later," *Proceedings
     of the National Academy of Sciences* 108, no. 36 (2011): 14998–15003, doi:10.1073/
     pnas.1108561108; National Institute of Mental Health Child Psychiatry Branch, *Press Release:
     Brain Matures a Few Years Late in ADHD, But Follows Normal Pattern* (November 2007), http://
     www.nih.gov/news/pr/nov2007/nimh-12.htm.

2   Jeree Pawl, "Being Held in Another's Mind," in *Concepts for Care: 20 Essays on Infant/Toddler
     Development and Learning*, eds. J. Ronald Lally, Peter L. Mangione, and Deborah Greenwald
     (San Francisco: WestEd, 2006): 1–5.

3   C. Rees, "Childhood Attachment," *The British Journal of General Practice* 57, no. 544 (2007): 920–22.

4   See "The History of Child Psychology," on *Essortment*, http://www.essortment.com/all/
     historyofchi_ribu.htm (accessed July 1, 2015).

5   John B. Watson, *Behaviorism* (New York: People's Institute Publishing Company, 1924), 104.

CHAPTER 2

1   Jeree Pawl, "Being Held in Another's Mind," in *Concepts for Care: 20 Essays on Infant/Toddler
     Development and Learning*, eds. J. Ronald Lally, Peter L. Mangione, and Deborah Greenwald
     (San Francisco: WestEd, 2006): 1–5.

2   Maureen Salamon, "11 Interesting Effects of Oxytocin," http://www.livescience.com/35219-
     11-effects-of-oxytocin.html (accessed June 15, 2015).

3   Robert Martone, "Scientists Discover Children's Cells Living in Mothers' Brain," *Scientific
     American*, http://www.scientificamerican.com/article/scientists-discover-childrens-cells-
     living-in-mothers-brain/ (accessed March 6, 2015).

4   Inge Bretherton, "The Origins of Attachment Theory: John Bowlby and Mary Ainsworth,"
    in *A Century of Developmental Psychology*, eds. Ross D. Parke, Peter A. Ornstein, et al.
    (Washington, DC: American Psychological Association, 1994): 431–71. Originally published
    in *Developmental Psychology* 28 (1992): 759–75.

5   Michelle M. Loman and Megan R. Gunnar, "Early Experience and the Development of
    Stress Reactivity and Regulation in Children," *Neuroscience & Biobehavioral Reviews* 34, no. 6
    (2010): 867–76, http://www.ncbi.nlm.nih.gov/pmc/articles/PMC2848877/ (accessed March 5,
    2015); Megan R. Gunnar and Philip A. Fisher, "Bringing Basic Research on Early Experience
    and Stress Neurobiology to Bear on Preventive Interventions for Neglected and Maltreated
    Children," *Development and Psychopathology* 18 (2006): 651–77, http://www.npc.umich.edu/
    news/events/early_life_2009/papers/ele_final_gunnar_et_al.pdf (accessed March 5, 2015).

6   D.O. Hebb, *The Organization of Behavior* (New York: Wiley & Sons, 1949).

7   Alison B. Wismer Fries, Elizabeth A. Shirtcliff, and Seth D. Pollak, "Neuroendocrine
    Dysregulation Following Early Social Deprivation in Children," *Developmental Psychobiology*
    50, no. 6 (2008): 588–99, doi:10.1002/dev.20319 and http://www.ncbi.nlm.nih.gov/pmc/
    articles/PMC2673795/.

8   Gunnar and Fisher, "Bringing Basic Research on Early Experience and Stress Neurobiology
    to Bear on Preventive Interventions for Neglected and Maltreated Children," 651–77.

9   Harriet S. Waters and Everett Waters, "The Attachment Working Models Concept: Among
    Other Things, We Build Script-Like Representations of Secure Base Experience," *Attachment
    & Human Development* 8, no. 3 (2006): 185–97, doi:10.1080/14616730600856016.

10 Bruce D. Perry, "Applying Principles of Neurodevelopment to Clinical Work with Maltreated and
    Traumatized Children: The Neurosequential Model of Therapeutics," in *Working with Traumatized
    Youth in Child Welfare*, ed. Nancy Boyd Webb (New York: Guildford Press, 2006): 27–52.

11 Laura E. Brumariu and Kathryn Kerns, "Parent–Child Attachment and Internalizing
    Symptoms in Childhood and Adolescence: A Review of Empirical Findings and
    Future Directions," *Development and Psychopathology* 22 (2010): 177–203, doi:10.1017/
    S0954579409990344; A. Lee and Benjamin L. Hankin, "Insecure Attachment, Dysfunctional
    Attitudes, and Low Self-Esteem Predicting Prospective Symptoms of Depression and Anxiety
    During Adolescence," *Journal of Clinical Child and Adolescent Psychology* 32, no. 2 (2009):
    219–31, doi:10.1080/15374410802698396; Kathryn A. Kerns, Michelle M. Abraham, et
    al., "Mother-Child Attachment in Later Middle Childhood: Assessment Approaches and
    Associations with Mood and Emotion Regulation," *Attachment & Human Development* 9, no. 1
    (2007): 33–53.

CHAPTER 3

1   Bruce D. Perry, "Childhood Experience and the Expression of Genetic Potential: What
    Childhood Neglect Tells Us about Nature and Nurture," *Brain and Mind* 3 (2002): 95.

2   See the following video link for an explanation of Dr. Gordon Neufeld's "mixing bowl"
    analogy: http://www.kidsinthehouse.com/preschooler/behavior-and-discipline/impulse-
    control/dealing-with-impulsive-behavior (accessed June 21, 2015).

3 For an excellent read on all things to do with teen development, see Dr. Daniel J. Siegel, *Brainstorm: The Power and Purpose of the Teenage Brain* (New York: Tarcher, 2014).

CHAPTER 4

1 http://circleofsecurity.net/news/circle-of-security-animation-video/ (accessed January 27, 2015).
2 http://boardofwisdom.com/togo/Quotes/ShowQuote?msgid=48030#.VQpfNWZRXj4.
3 D.W. Winnicott, *The Child, the Family, and the Outside World* (London: Penguin, 1973).

CHAPTER 5

1 Roger Thompson, "The Scientific Evidence against Spanking, Timeouts, and Sleep Training," *Quartz* (December 18, 2014), http://qz.com/310622/the-scientific-evidence-against-spanking-timeouts-and-sleep-training/ (accessed February 2, 2015).
2 W.W. Dyer, *Staying on the Path* (Carlsbad, CA: Hay House Inc, 2004): 144. Kindle edition. See also Wayne Dyer's Facebook page: https://www.facebook.com/drwaynedyer/posts/10151866740351030 (accessed August 31, 2015).
3 Brigid Schulte, *Overwhelmed: How to Work, Love, and Play When No One Has the Time* (New York: Picador, 2014).
4 David Elkind, "The Power of Play: Learning What Comes Naturally," *American Journal of Play* 1, no. 1 (Summer 2008): 1–6.

CHAPTER 6

1 Christine Schwartz, Charlotte Waddell, et al., "Parenting without Physical Punishment," *Children's Mental Health Research Quarterly* 9, no. 1 (Vancouver: Children's Health Policy Centre, Faculty of Health Sciences, Simon Fraser University, 2015): 1–16.

CHAPTER 7

1 Debi Gliori, *No Matter What* (San Diego, CA: HMH Books for Young Readers, 2008).
2 D.O. Hebb, *The Organization of Behavior* (New York: Wiley & Sons, 1949).
3 Bruce D. Perry, "Applying Principles of Neurodevelopment to Clinical Work with Maltreated and Traumatized Children: The Neurosequential Model of Therapeutics," in *Working with Traumatized Youth in Child Welfare*, ed. Nancy Boyd Webb (New York: Guildford Press, 2006): 27–52.

CHAPTER 8

1 As quoted in Karl Iglesias, *The 101 Habits of Highly Successful Screenwriters: Insider Secrets from Hollywood's Top Writers* (Fairfield, OH: Adams Media, 2001): 4.
2 Bruce D. Perry, and Ronnie Pollard, "Homeostasis, Stress, Trauma, and Adaptation: A Neurodevelopmental View of Childhood Trauma," *Child and Adolescent Psychiatric Clinics of North America* 7, no. 1 (January 1998): 33–51.
3 Kittie Frantz, "Doesn't the Breast Work Anymore?," *Mothering* 132 (September/October 2005): 50.
4 Carl J. Dunst, Charlie Johanson, et al., "Family-oriented Early Intervention Policies and Practices: Family-centered or Not?," *Exceptional Children* 58, no. 2 (1991): 115–26.

ACKNOWLEDGMENTS

The arrival of this book comes as part of a wonderful journey full of experiences and people who have supported, challenged, and championed it into being. Its origins go back several years and have thus been influenced by a brilliantly eclectic group of people along the way. I am most delighted to have a chance here to acknowledge the many shining stars in this group.

I am beyond grateful to Maggie Langrick, President & Publisher of LifeTree Media, for quite literally making this book be so. I felt your confidence from that fateful first coffee meeting, and it was truly what sustained me in seeing this project through to fruition. Your ability to quietly "be" makes you a special big person of the greatest magnitude. And to the amazing team at LifeTree Media that jumped onboard for the ride with enthusiasm and expertise, your collective impact in the work you are doing is life changing for the trickle-down effect it creates in the dissemination of material so important to our world. Specifically, I have oceans of gratitude for Michelle MacAleese, my steadfast and inspired editor. From our first "date" to the completion of this project, you found a way into my mind and my message. Your ability to "just know" and your respect for both me and my topic filled me up. You are a true master at your craft, and your suggestions big and small elevated something good to something really special. You are valued beyond words. To Paris Spence-Lang, marketing coordinator, you've got sparkle! And you deliver advice, know-how, and direction in all you do in a manner that left me utterly secure in the knowledge that I was in the best of hands. Thank you for making that so easy. To Ingrid Paulson, designer, you are a magician. That you could find visual ways to convey the complexity of my thoughts and allow this work to have presence beyond its words is a feat for which I have immense respect. Thank you for sharing your talents with me. I am also grateful to Lucy Kenward, copyeditor. You very quickly "got" my ideas! Thank you for adeptly providing a resolutely informed and thorough review of my work, taking the final product to even greater heights. To Margaret MacKinnon-Cash, a person of many talents who stepped in swiftly and capably to the role of managing editor, thank you for your absolute and enthusiastic support of this project. Additional thanks to Stephen Ullstrom, proofer and indexer. The level of detail your mind can lock onto is extraordinary and I felt your "hulk" quality as you capably tightened the final product. And to all of the others on the LifeTree team quietly working alongside, thank you for your effort and for your commitment to helping authors like myself find their voice.

Beyond the writing and creation of this book, invaluable publicity support has made its contents known, allowing my purpose of "changing the conversation" to actually happen! To that end I thank Beth Gebhard, Heather Adams, and Maggie Rheney of Choice Media and Communications, along with the rest of their team, for American publicity support. You believed in this project from "hello," and your genuine embrace of my ideas and absolute warmth of character made you valued kindred spirits. And to Margaret MacKinnon-Cash of LifeTree Media, I am grateful for your additional role in supplying expert knowledge and creating key connections in providing Canadian publicity support. That you wholeheartedly scooped up my message and facilitated its dissemination means much to me. Thank you to both Choice and Margaret for helping me connect to the world so that a new conversation about children can begin.

There are many others who have taken my hand and come alongside as this project took shape. Amongst them, I give a big, warm, cozy thank you to the magnificent Lindsay Faber of Lindsay Faber Photography for knowing just how to capture me. Your friendship and support make my world go 'round. To Tara Mihalech, you rescued me in the crazy virtual world at exactly the moment I needed you most! You have wit, skill, and kindness all wrapped up in the best possible package. Thank you for jumping in with such confidence. I am indebted. To Rebecca Mitchell, my colleague and ultimate supporter, your confident, steadfast presence; unwavering belief in me; and uncanny knack for selecting the perfect wine for any of our "meetings" (right, Jeff?!) are all part of what makes life feel good. Adore you! To Natalie Rocke Henderson, a colleague of the utmost skill and the biggest heart, you have been there from the start, through babies and dissertations to now, and have always had my back. Thank you, friend. To Pamela Chatry, friend and business advisor, I am full of appreciation for all that you have done for me, not the least of which was literally planting the seed for this book project and confidently suggesting that the time was now. Change is good, Donkey! To Dr. Martha Foschi, my professor and mentor, for believing in me and in so doing, inspiring me to believe in myself. Your impact on my professional development has ripple effects that will continue for all of time. To Ms. Wendy Neifer, whose strength of character and ability to inspire the drive for such in myself had an enduring impact in shaping who I am today. To Dr. Parm Rai at Rai Chiropractic; Kenny Hagerty at Physiomoves; and Laura, Yossi, and crew at the Hit—you physically made this possible, for without your most amazing care and expertise, my physical self may not have endured! Who knew keyboarding was such a taxing sport?! Oh, Vanessa.

There are also several groups of important individuals to whom I owe so much. To the British Columbia Infant Development Program, and especially Dana Brynelsen, thank you for welcoming me into your midst during my most formative years, and in so doing, wonderfully altering the course of all that was to come for me. And to the British Columbia Supported Child Development program, other early intervention programs, agencies, and therapists, and all of the amazing big people who work determinedly for the children and families of our communities, I am in your debt for the sharing of knowledge and passion. As well, to the countless professionals and parents who have attended my workshops, asked tough questions, and inspired throughout, I am grateful to you for pushing me to new understanding and appreciation of what it is to "be." And to the amazing team at The Wishing Star Developmental Clinic who have championed me in every way but, most importantly, who have inspired me in the way that you work so tirelessly and compassionately for all of "our" children. I adore you.

In all of this, I reserve a very special thank you for the families and children that I have had the extraordinary privilege to walk alongside. You are heroes in my eyes. I have learned much from you and am in awe of your reserves. I am eternally grateful for the opportunity to be part of your journey, and humbled by your trust as you welcomed me into your inner circle. For the big people in this collective, your children are lucky to have you. For the little people in this collective, you shine so brightly and so bravely. Please come back for tea when you are thirty-seven!

And finally, thank you to all of you who are part of my inner circle. To the many friends and families in our "village" who create an everyday world for my family and I that is manageable, sprinkled with joy, and full of life, I am wrapping you all up right now in a giant hug of gratitude. To my extended family, who have cared for our children, cooked meals, rushed over for unexpected school pickups, and generally looked after us, none of this would have been possible without you. To my "fourth" sister, Kateryna Holub, who sailed down the escalator at YVR 6 years ago to land right in my heart and that of our family, you will never know how much I cherish your friendship, spirit, generosity, humor, and enduring presence. You are one in a million. To Fonny-b-nonny, a special kind of big person for my 2 special little people, your intuition and love for humanity comes straight from the heart, and I am so thankful to know you live in the neurons of our boys! I am also grateful to my beautiful sisters, Lisa, Christy, and Laurel, who each bring special gifts and their own unique presence to my life. Even across the miles, every text, messenger chat, phone call, and email has our connection endure. Love you all. To my parents, thank you. My wish for you is that you will know the depth of the trickle-down in all of the little things you have done and said across my 4 decades in being my cherished big people. The enormity of that influence is impossible to adequately capture with words, so I send you my deepest gratitude via the twinkly reality of your influence in the life I love living today. Thank you for "just knowing." And finally, heartfelt thanks to all 3 of my beautiful boys. Nathan and Maxwell, being your big person is my greatest privilege and most resounding joy. I am so proud and so lucky to have you call me mom. Jonathan, you are the partner that many dream of. Your ability to flow into the nooks and crannies of our life and support, fill in, cover, understand, cherish, and just "be" is incredible. To the 3 of you who have given so freely of your love and precious time to have this project unfold, I love you beyond measure.

INDEX

Dr. Vanessa Lapointe is a registered psychologist (British Columbia #1856) who has been supporting families and children for more than fifteen years. She presently works in private practice and has previous experience in a variety of settings, including the British Columbia Ministry of Children and Family Development and the school system. Dr. Vanessa's passion is in walking alongside parents, teachers, care providers, and other big people to really see the world through the child's eyes. She believes that if we can do this, we are beautifully positioned to grow up our children in the best possible way. A regularly invited educator and speaker, and a consultant to research projects and various organizations promoting emotional health and development, Dr. Vanessa is known for bringing a sense of nurturing understanding and humanity to all of her work. As a mother to 2 growing children, Dr. Vanessa strives not only professionally, but also personally, to view the world through the child's eyes.